The Great American Citizenship Quiz

The Great American Citizenship Quiz

NEWLY REVISED AND UPDATED

....

Can You Pass Your Own Country's Citizenship Test?

....

SOLOMON M. SKOLNICK

B L O O M S B U R Y

NEW YORK • LONDON • OXFORD • NEW DELHI • SYDNEY

Bloomsbury USA
An imprint of Bloomsbury Publishing Plc

1385 Broadway, New York, NY 10018 USA
50 Bedford Square, London, WC1B 3DP UK

www.bloomsbury.com

BLOOMSBURY and the Diana logo are trademarks of Bloomsbury Publishing Plc

First published 2009
This paperback edition 2017

ISBN: PB: 978-1-63557-015-1
         ePub: 978-1-63557-016-8

LIBRARY OF CONGRESS CATALOGING-IN-PUBLICATION DATA

Skolnick, Solomon M.
  The great American citizenship quiz / Solomon M. Skolnick.—3rd ed.
    p. cm.
  Includes bibliographical references and index.
  ISBN: 978-1-63557-015-1 (alk. paper)
  1. Citizenship—United States. I. Title.
JK1759.S62 2009
323.6076—dc22

                                                              2009019187

4 6 8 10 9 7 5

Typeset by Rachel Reiss
Printed and bound in the U.S.A. by Sheridan, Chelsea, Michigan

To find out more about our authors and books visit www.bloomsbury.com. Here
you will find extracts, author interviews, details of forthcoming events, and the
option to sign up for our newsletters.

Bloomsbury books may be purchased for business or promotional use. For
information on bulk purchases please contact Macmillan Corporate and Premium
Sales Department at specialmarkets@macmillan.com.

Contents

. . . .

Introduction

· ·

*Citizenship: The status of a citizen with its attendant
duties, rights, and privileges.*
——*American Heritage Dictionary*

AT OUR NATION's beginnings freedom itself was con-
tradictory: The craftsmen of our freedom, who had
shaken off their own masters, could be masters of other
men and denied their own mothers, wives, and daugh-
ters the right to vote. But the founders, despite their
shortcomings, were driven to create a most extraordinary crucible of freedom and opportunity, which has
been sustained by the remarkable depth of their beliefs
and courage. The ability of the founders to articulate
the workings of democracy in the documents that they
drafted and the resilient institutions that they created
have endured through slavery and prejudice, war and
catastrophe, to provide compassion and forgiveness,
inspiration and hope.

During the last decade the U.S. Citizenship and Immigration Services (USCIS) has welcomed more than
6.6 million naturalized citizens into our nation.

The Great American Citizenship Quiz provides the complete test and more. For those of you who are history
buffs, and for those taking the test who want deeper
detail, we have added fascinating background material,
text of original documents, as well as quizzes, stories,

and facts about our government and society, which have now thrived for more than two centuries.

The Great American Citizenship Quiz reflects the test's emphasis on identifying and teaching basic American ideas, values, rights, and responsibilities. Prospective citizens will be asked to answer up to ten of a potential one hundred questions. The text of the one hundred questions and the possible accepted answers reproduced here are provided by the U.S. Citizenship and Immigration Services.

THE QUIZ

. . . .

⭐ The Four Ideals, also known as self-evident truths, extolled in the Declaration of Independence are equality, natural rights, consent of the governed, and the right to revolution.

These are the times that try men's souls. The summer soldier and the sunshine patriot will, in this crisis, shrink from the service of the country; but he that stands it now deserves the love and thanks of man and woman. Tyranny, like hell, is not easily conquered, yet we have this consolation with us, that the harder the conflict the more glorious the triumph. What we obtain too cheap we esteem too lightly; it is dearness only that gives everything its value.
—Thomas Paine, *Common Sense*, 1776

America is the only nation in the world that is founded on a creed. Other nations find their identity and cohesion in ethnicity, or geography, or partisan ideology, or cultural tradition. But America was founded on certain ideas—ideas about freedom, about human dignity, and about social responsibility.
—G. K. Chesterton, *What I Saw in America*, 1922

Civil liberties emphasizes the liberty of the individual. In many other forms of government the importance of the individual has disappeared. The individual lives for the state. Here in a democracy the government still exists for the individual, but that does not mean that we do not have to watch and that we do not have to examine ourselves to be sure that we preserve the civil liberties for all our people, which are the basis of our democracy.

—Eleanor Roosevelt, March 14, 1940

Prudence, indeed, will dictate that governments long established, should not be changed for light and transient causes; and, accordingly, all experience [has] shown that mankind are more disposed to suffer while evils are sufferable than to right themselves by abolishing the forms to which they are accustomed. But, when a long train of abuses and usurpations, pursuing invariably the same object, evinces a design to reduce [the people] under absolute despotism, it is their right, it is their duty, to throw off such government, and to provide new guards for their future security.

—Thomas Jefferson, Declaration of Independence

AMERICAN GOVERNMENT

. . . .

PRINCIPLES OF AMERICAN DEMOCRACY

1 What is the supreme law of the land?

. . . .

☞ *the Constitution*

. . . .

2 What does the Constitution do?

. . . .

☞ *sets up the government, defines the government, protects basic rights of Americans*

. . . .

3 The idea of self-government is in the first three words of the Constitution. What are these words?

. . . .

☞ *We the People*

. . . .

THE CONSTITUTION, THE cornerstone of the American government, describes the structure of the government and the rights of "we the people": "We the People of the United States, in Order to form a more perfect Union, establish Justice, insure domestic Tranquility, provide for the common defense, promote the general Welfare, and secure the Blessings of Liberty to ourselves and our Posterity, do ordain and establish this Constitution for the United States of America." No law may be passed that contradicts its principles, and no person, or the government, is exempt from following it.

4   What is an amendment?

. . . .

☞   *a change (to the Constitution), an addition (to the Constitution)*

. . . .

THE CONSTITUTION CAN be amended by two methods. By the first method, both the Senate and the House

⭐ *The U.S. Constitution doesn't guarantee happiness, only the pursuit of it. You have to catch up with it your self.*

—Benjamin Franklin

The original Constitution is on display in the Rotunda for the Charters of Freedom in the National Archives in Washington D.C., which also houses the Declaration of Independence and the Bill of Rights.

must pass a bill by a two-thirds majority. The bill then goes from Congress to the individual states. Amendments must have the approval of the legislatures or conventions of three-fourths of the states before they become part of the Constitution. The second method, which has never been used, requires that a constitutional convention be called by at least two-thirds of the legislatures of the states, and calls for that convention to propose one or more amendments. These amendments would then be sent to the states to be approved by three-fourths of the legislatures or conventions.

The president has no role in the amendment process. The president cannot veto an amendment proposal or a ratification.

5   **What do we call the first ten amendments to the Constitution?**

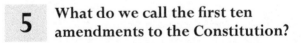 *The Bill of Rights*

6   **What is one right or freedom from the First Amendment?**

⭐ *The very aim and end of our institutions is just this: that we may think what we like and say what we think.*

—Oliver Wendell Holmes

I tell them I have worked 40 years to make the Women's suffrage platform broad enough for Atheists and Agnostics to stand upon, and now if need be I will fight the next 40 to keep it Catholic enough to permit the straightest Orthodox religionist to speak or pray and count her beads upon.

—Susan B. Anthony

If you want to be free, there is but one way; it is to guarantee an equally full measure of liberty to all your neighbors. There is no other.

—Carl Shurz

The free press is the mother of all our liberties and of our progress under liberty.

—Adlai E. Stevenson

Congress shall make no law respecting an establishment of religion, or prohibiting the free exercise thereof; or abridging the freedom of speech, or the press, or the right of the people peaceably to assemble, and to petition the Government for a redress of grievances.

—First Amendment to the Constitution

. . . .

☞ *speech, religion, assembly, press, petition the government*

. . . .

THE BILL OF Rights wasn't included in the version of the Constitution that was sent to the states for ratification on September 28, 1787. The lack of such an enumeration of rights, which some feared would open the way to tyranny by the central government, led two delegates, George Mason and Elbridge Gerry, to refuse to sign the Constitution.

By September 1789 there was an increasing urgency regarding the creation and adoption of a Bill of Rights. This was prompted in large part by the demand for such a bill by the states during the ratification process. Some of these states had granted only conditional ratification based on the near-future inclusion of such rights as part of the Constitution. In response the First Congress of the United States proposed twelve amendments, only nine months after the new government under the Constitution formally went into effect on March 4, 1789. Ten of those amendments, which spell out the privileges and immunities of individual citizens, became the Bill of Rights.

7 **How many amendments does the Constitution have?**

☞ *twenty-seven (27)*

8 **What did the Declaration of Independence do?**

☞ *announced our independence (from Great Britain), declared our independence (from*

Great Britain), said that the United States is
free (from Great Britain)

. . . .

9 What are two rights in the Declaration of Independence?

. . . .

☞ *life, liberty, pursuit of happiness*

. . . .

10 What is freedom of religion?

. . . .

☞ *You can practice any religion, or not practice*
a religion.

. . . .

⭐ *Freedom to differ is not limited to things that do not matter much. That would be a mere shadow of freedom. The test of freedom's substance is the right to differ as to things that touch the heart of the existing order. If there is any fixed star in our constitutional constellation, it is that no official, high or petty, can prescribe what shall be orthodox in politics, nationalism, religion, or other matters of opinion, or force citizens to confess by word or act their faith within.*

—Supreme Court Justice Robert Jackson

11 What is the economic system in the United States?

☞ *capitalist economy, market economy*

12 What is the "rule of law"?

☞ *everyone must follow the law; leaders must obey the law; government must obey the law; no one is above the law*

SYSTEM OF GOVERNMENT

13 Name one branch or part of the government.

☞ *Congress, legislative, president, executive, the courts, judicial*

14 What stops one branch of government from becoming too powerful?

☞ *checks and balances, separation of powers*

THE PRESIDENT'S POWER is checked by the Congress, which can refuse to confirm his appointees and has the power to impeach, or remove, a president. Congress passes laws, but the president must sign them or he may veto them. Congress has a mechanism to override a veto. And the Supreme Court may rule on the constitutionality of a law, but Congress, with approval from two-thirds of the states, may amend the Constitution.

15 Who is in charge of the executive branch?

. . . .

☞   *the president*

. . . .

THE RESPONSIBILITY OF the executive branch is to ensure that laws are carried out and enforced. It is charged with operating the business of government, overseeing national security, and representing the United States' political and economic interests on the international stage.

The Constitution requires that the president must meet all three of these requirements: be a natural-born citizen of the United States; be at least thirty-five years old; and have lived in the United States for at least fourteen years.

The founders believed that these criteria would ensure that the man in the office (women could not vote, let alone hold elected office, until the ratification of the Nineteenth Amendment of the Constitution in 1920) understood the nature of the country and had sufficient life experience to serve it well. The vice president, who

> ⭐ However much we may differ in the choice of the measures which should guide the administration of the government, there can be but little doubt in the minds of those who are really friendly to the republican features of our system that one of its most important securities consists in the separation of the legislative and executive powers at the same time that each is acknowledged to be supreme, in the will of the people constitutionally expressed.
>
> —Andrew Jackson

> "The framers of our Constitution lived among the ruins of a system of intermingled legislative and judicial powers" in which colonial legislatures routinely meddled in judicial functions. The framers created separated powers as a "structural safeguard" against such abuses, he said, "establishing high walls and clear distinctions because low walls and vague distinctions will not be judicially defensible in the heat of interbranch conflict."
>
> —Linda Greenhouse, quoting
> Justice John Scalia, *New York Times*

sits only a heartbeat away from the presidency, must meet the same criteria.

16 Who makes federal laws?

· ·

 Congress, Senate and House (of Representatives), (U.S. or national) legislature

· ·

17 What are the two parts of the U.S. Congress?

☞   *the Senate and House (of Representatives)*

THE LEGISLATIVE BRANCH is charged with creating laws. Article I of the Constitution established Congress, the legislative body made up of the Senate and the House. The primary function of Congress is to write, debate, and pass bills and to send them on to the president for his approval or veto.

18 How many U.S. senators are there?

☞   *one hundred (100)*

19 We elect a U.S. senator for how many years?

☞   *six (6)*

A SENATOR MUST be at least thirty years of age, have been a citizen of the United States for nine years, and, when elected, be a resident of the state from which he or she is chosen. There are no limits to the number of terms that a senator may serve.

Can you match the accomplishment with the senator?

1. A former First Lady who became a U.S. Senator from New York, became Secretary of State, and was the first woman to run for president as the nominee of a major party.

2. The first Hispanic senator: 1928.

3. The first woman elected to the Senate. The governor of Arkansas appointed her to the seat left vacant by the death of her husband assuming that she would hold it only until the next election. Instead, she ran for the office and won an upset victory in 1932. She was subsequently re-elected twice, serving until 1945.

4. The first Native American senator: 1907.

5. The first African American to be elected to the Senate: 1870.

6. The first African American woman elected to the Senate: 1993

7. The first woman to serve in both houses of Congress. The first woman to actively seek the presidential nomination of a major party.

8. The first woman to be appointed and serve in the Senate: 1922.

9. The only person to represent three states in the U.S. Senate: he represented Illinois from 1849 to 1855, Minnesota from 1858 to 1859, and Missouri in 1879.

10. The longest serving senator, having been first elected in 1959. He served fifty-one years, five months, and twenty-six days.

A. Hiram R. Revels

B. Robert C. Byrd

C. James Shields

D. Octaviano Larrazollo

F. Rebecca Felton

G. Margaret Chase Smith

H. Hattie Ophelia Wyatt Caraway

I. Hillary Rodham Clinton

J. Carol Moseley-Braun

K. Charles Curtis

ANSWERS: 1-I, 2-D, 3-H, 4-K, 5-A, 6-J, 7-G, 8-F, 9-C, 10-B

20 Who is one of your state's U.S. senators?

☞ *Answers will vary. [For District of Columbia residents and residents of U.S. territories, the answer is that D.C. (or the territory where the applicant lives) has no U.S. senators.] Please see Appendix B, page 105, for the complete list of current U.S. senators.*

21 The House of Representatives has how many voting members?

☞ *four hundred thirty-five (435)*

THERE ARE 435 representatives (called congressmen or congresswomen) in the House of Representatives. The number of House members increased as the population expanded through 1913, when 435 became the set number of members. The House also has nonvoting "delegates" from the District of Columbia, American Samoa, Guam, the U.S. Virgin Islands, and a "resident commissioner" from Puerto Rico.

A congressional district is comprised of about 660,000 people. There are seven states with only one representative: Alaska, Delaware, Montana, North Dakota, South Dakota, Vermont, and Wyoming, giving these states fewer seats in the more populous House than they have in the Senate.

22 We elect a U.S. representative for how many years?

☞ *two (2)*

THERE ARE NO limits on the number of terms a representative can serve. Since the entire House of Representatives is elected every two years, a "new" Congress convenes every two years, in the January following a November election. The first Congress convened in 1789.

23 Name your U.S. representative.

☞ *Answers will vary. [Residents of territories with nonvoting delegates or resident commissioners may provide the name of that delegate or commissioner. Also acceptable is any statement that the territory has no (voting) representatives in Congress.] Please see Appendix C, page 108 for the complete list of current U.S. representatives.*

24 Whom does a U.S. senator represent?

☞ *all people of the state*

25 Why do some states have more representatives than other states?

☞ because of the state's populations, because they have more people, because some states have more people

ROGER SHERMAN, A delegate from Connecticut to the Constitutional Convention, is credited with the creation of the Great Compromise, which established equal representation for each state in the Senate and representation relative to population size in the House of Representatives, thereby responding to the concerns of both the large and small states.

26 We elect a president for how many years?

☞ *four (4)*

UNTIL THE TWENTY-SECOND Amendment to the Constitution was ratified on February 27, 1951, there were no term limits for the president. The two-term maximum was a tradition but not a law. George Washington "retired" after two terms, and his successors were clear about their belief, as articulated by Thomas Jefferson, that "If some termination to the services of the chief Magistrate be not fixed by the Constitution, or supplied by practice, his office, nominally four years, will in fact become for life."

The Twenty-second Amendment states that no person may be elected president more than twice. The vice president or another person who succeeds to the presidency, and serves as president or acting president for more than two years, may not be elected president more than once. The maximum length of time one person may serve as president is ten consecutive years. That person would first succeed to the presidency and sterve for no more than two years, and then be elected to two full four-year terms.

Franklin D. Roosevelt was the only president to be elected more than twice. He died in office in April 1945 at the beginning of his fourth term, having served for more than twelve years. Harry S. Truman, his successor, who was president when the Twenty-second Amendment passed Congress in 1947, was the last president eligible to run for a third term.

27 In what month do we vote for president?

....

☞ *November*

....

NOVEMBER WAS CHOSEN because it was felt that harvest time (in the largely agrarian United States of the time) would be over and men would be able to leave rural areas to travel to their polling places. Elections are held on a Tuesday to give voters time to travel on Monday, since Sunday was generally a day for church attendance.

The law establishing the first uniform election day, to guarantee the simultaneous selection of the electors in all states, was passed by Congress in 1845. From 1792 to

1845 elections could be held on different days and dates in each state provided that they completed the selection of their electors anytime within a thirty-four-day period before the first Wednesday of December.

The Constitution established March 4 as Inauguration Day in order to allow sufficient time for officials to gather and count election returns by hand and for newly elected officeholders to travel to the capital. When March 4 fell on a Sunday, as it did in 1821, 1849, 1877, and 1917, the ceremonies were held on March 5.

George Washington's first inauguration did not take place until April 30, 1789. Although it was scheduled for March 4, additional time was needed to actually count the ballots, which made it necessary to give the president-elect more time to travel from his home in Mount Vernon, Virginia, to the capital in New York City.

By the early part of the twentieth century, modern transportation and communication devices rendered the three-month transition period anachronistic. The Twentieth Amendment to the Constitution, ratified in 1933, moved the inauguration date to January 20. Franklin D. Roosevelt was the last president to be inaugurated on March 4 (1933) and the first president to be inaugurated in January.

28   What is the name of the president of the United States now?

· ·

☞   *Donald J. Trump, Donald Trump, Trump*

· ·

THE PRESIDENTS, PRIOR to Donald Trump, were:

1. George Washington (1789–97) 2. John Adams (1797–1801) 3. Thomas Jefferson (1801–09) 4. James Madison (1809–17) 5. James Monroe (1817–25) 6. John Quincy Adams (1825–29) 7. Andrew Jackson (1829–37) 8. Martin Van Buren (1837–41) 9. William Henry Harrison (March 4–April 4, 1841) 10. John Tyler (1841–45) 11. James K. Polk (1845–49) 12. Zachary Taylor (1849–50) 13. Millard Fillmore (1850–53) 14. Franklin Pierce (1853–57) 15. James Buchanan (1857–61) 16. Abraham Lincoln (1861–65) 17. Andrew Johnson (1865–69) 18. Ulysses S. Grant (1869–77) 19. Rutherford B. Hayes (1877–81) 20. James Garfield (March 4–September 19, 1881) 21. Chester A. Arthur (1881–85) 22. Grover Cleveland (1885–89) 23. Benjamin Harrison (1889–93) 24. Grover Cleveland (1893–97) 25. William McKinley (1897–1901) 26. Theodore Roosevelt (1901–09) 27. William Howard Taft (1909–13) 28. Woodrow Wilson (1913–21) 29. Warren G. Harding (1921–23) 30. Calvin Coolidge (1923–29) 31. Herbert Hoover (1929–33) 32. Franklin D. Roosevelt (1933–45) 33. Harry S. Truman (1945–53) 34. Dwight D. Eisenhower (1953–61) 35. John F. Kennedy (1961–63) 36. Lyndon Baines Johnson (1963–69) 37. Richard M. Nixon (1969–74) 38. Gerald R. Ford (1974–77) 39. Jimmy Carter (1977–81) 40. Ronald Reagan (1981–89) 41. George H. W. Bush (1989–93) 42. William Jefferson (Bill) Clinton (1993–2001) 43. George W. Bush (2001–2009) 44. Barack Obama (2009–2017)

George Washington and city planner Pierre L'Enfant chose the site for the presidential residence, and architect James Hoban created the design. The first official name of the residence was the President's House and later the Executive Mansion. It first took on its now-familiar color in 1798 because of the limestone whitewash that was applied to protect the exterior from freezing as it was being built. John and Abigail Adams were the first to occupy the residence, while it was still under construction in 1800. It survived a fire at the hands of the British in 1814 (during the War of 1812). It has been popularly referred to as the White House since the early 1800s, but President Theodore Roosevelt made the White House the official name of the residence in 1901.

The White House contains the living quarters for the president and the president's family, and offices for the president and the president's staff. There are 132 rooms in the fifty-five-thousand-square-foot structure located on eighteen acres of land. The West Wing was built in 1902 during the administration of Theodore Roosevelt. The Oval Office, which we now think of as synonymous with the office of president, was built for William

⭐ **PRESIDENTIAL FAMILY TIES**

- George W. Bush is the son of George H. W. Bush.
- John Quincy Adams was the son of John Adams.
- Benjamin Harrison was the grandson of William Henry Harrison.
- James Madison and Zachary Taylor were second cousins.
- Franklin Delano Roosevelt was distantly related to eleven U.S. presidents, five by blood and six by marriage: John Adams, John Quincy Adams, Ulysses S. Grant, Benjamin Harrison, William Henry Harrison, James Madison, Theodore Roosevelt, William Howard Taft, Zachary Taylor, Martin Van Buren, and the father of us all, George Washington.

Howard Taft, who first used it in 1909, more than a century after John Adams first moved in.

29 What is the name of the vice president of the United States now?

· ·

☞ *Mike Pence, Michael Richard Pence, Pence*

· ·

THE JOB THAT John Adams, the first vice president, described as "the most insignificant office that ever the invention of man contrived or his imagination conceived" has only one constitutionally mandated duty (Article I, Section 3): to serve as the president of the Senate. The Constitution (Article II, Section 1) also provides for the vice president to take over the duties of the president should the president be incapacitated or die.

From 1789 to 1804 the presidential candidate with the most electoral votes became president, and the runner-up became vice president. This plan to place the most qualified persons in the top two offices foundered as people of different political persuasions, who had been competing for the same office, often found themselves at odds with each other at the head of the executive branch of the government. In 1804 Congress passed the Twelfth Amendment to the Constitution, which created the concept of a "ticket" comprising one nominee for president and one for vice president from each political party.

The Twenty-fifth Amendment to the Constitution was ratified (1967) creating a procedure for filling a vacancy in the office of vice president: the president nominates a vice president and that nomination must be confirmed by a majority vote of both houses of Congress. The amendment came just in the nick of time. In 1973 Gerald R. Ford succeeded Spiro T. Agnew, who had resigned. One year later Ford, having succeeded to the presidency upon the resignation of Richard M. Nixon, chose New York governor Nelson A. Rockefeller as his vice president.

30 If the president can no longer serve, who becomes president?

. . . .

☞   *the vice president*

. . . .

FROM 1792 TO 1886, the president pro tempore of the Senate and the Speaker of the House were next in line after the vice president to succeed the president. This changed in 1886 when the leaders in Congress were replaced in the succession by cabinet officers, beginning with the secretary of state.

The Presidential Succession Act of 1947 established the Speaker of the House as the next in line after the vice president. The president pro tempore of the Senate is next, followed by the members of the cabinet in the order in which their respective departments were established. See page 76 for order of succession.

31 If both the president and the vice president can no longer serve, who becomes president?

. . . .

☞   *the Speaker of the House*

. . . .

⭐ What better way to prepare to become president than by first serving as vice president? Fourteen men who were vice president later became president: John Adams, Thomas Jefferson, Martin Van Buren, John Tyler, Millard Fillmore, Andrew Johnson, Chester A. Arthur, Theodore Roosevelt, Calvin Coolidge, Harry S. Truman, Lyndon Baines Johnson, Richard M. Nixon, Gerald Ford, and George H. W. Bush.

Can you match the vice president with his blunder?

A. Charged with treason for allegedly masterminding a plot to attack the Spanish colony of Mexico.

B. Known as the "Arch Nullifier" for his proposal, which was roundly rejected, to allow any one state to nullify an Act of Congress.

C. Believing that the planet was hollow, he proposed an expedition to the North Pole to drill to the center of the Earth.

D. While in office he complained to his wife that he was "the most unimportant man in Washington, ignored by the President, the cabinet, and Congress."

E. Shot and killed former Treasury Secretary Alexander Hamilton.

F. Declared that his greatest aspiration was "to make the world safe for corn breeders."

G. Told a bodyguard that his job was pointless because no one ever shoots a vice president.

1. John C. Calhoun
2. Hannibal Hamlin
3. Aaron Burr
4. Thomas Marshall
5. Richard M. Johnson
6. Henry Wallace

32 Who is the commander in chief of the military?

☞ *the president*

ACCORDING TO THE Constitution (Article II, Section 2), the president "shall be Commander in Chief of the Army and Navy of the United States, and of the Militia of the several States, when called into the actual Service of the United States."

33 Who signs bills to become laws?

☞ *the president*

34 Who vetoes bills?

☞ *the president*

⭐ Twelve presidents were generals prior to becoming commander in chief: George Washington, William Henry Harrison, Zachary Taylor, Andrew Johnson, Ulysses S. Grant, Rutherford B. Hayes, Benjamin Harrison, William Henry Harrison, Chester A. Arthur, James Garfield, Franklin Pierce, and Dwight D. Eisenhower.

35   What does the president's cabinet do?

☞   *advises the president*

36   What are two cabinet-level positions?

☞   *Secretary of Agriculture*
Secretary of Commerce
Secretary of Defense
Secretary of Education
Secretary of Energy
Secretary of Health and Human Services
Secretary of Homeland Security
Secretary of Housing and Urban Development
Secretary of Interior
Secretary of State
Secretary of Transportation
Secretary of Treasury
Secretary of Veterans' Affairs
Secretary of Labor
Attorney General

ALTHOUGH THE CABINET is not mentioned in the Constitution, Article II, Section 2 is cited as one of the rationales for its creation. It states that the president "may require the opinion, in writing of the principal officer in each of the executive departments, upon any subject relating to the duties of their respective offices."

Who's in the cabinet? Match the description with the person.

A. The first woman to be appointed attorney general (1993–2001), by President Bill Clinton.

B. Served as the U.S. Secretary of War (1853–57) and as the president of the Confederate States (1861–65).

C. The first woman appointed to the cabinet. She served as secretary of labor under Franklin D. Roosevelt beginning in 1933.

D. Was defeated for the Republican nomination for president by Abraham Lincoln and later served as his secretary of state.

E. Served as secretary of state (1829–31), vice president of the United States (1833–41), and president (1837–41).

F. The first African American to be appointed secretary of state (2001–05), by George W. Bush.

G. Was defeated for the Republican nomination for president by Abraham Lincoln and later served as his attorney general.

H. The first African American woman to be appointed secretary of state (2005–09), by George W. Bush.

I. Served as the vice president of the United States (1857–61) and as the secretary of war for the Confederate States (1865).

J. The first woman to be appointed secretary of state (1997–2001), by President Bill Clinton.

1. Condoleezza Rice
2. General Colin Powell
3. Martin Van Buren
4. John C. Breckenridge
5. William H. Seward
6. Frances Perkins
7. Jefferson Davis
8. Edward Bates
9. Madeline Albright
10. Janet Reno

Answers: A-10, B-7, C-6, D-5, E-3, F-2, G-8, H-1, I-4, J-9

28

Members are appointed by the president, subject to confirmation by a simple (fifty-one-vote) majority of the Senate. Their terms are not fixed, and they may be replaced at any time by the president. At a change in administration, it is customary for cabinet members to resign, but they remain in office until successors are appointed.

37 What does the judicial branch do?

· ·

☞   *reviews laws, explains laws, resolves disputes (disagreements), decides if a law goes against the Constitution*

· ·

38 What is the highest court in the United States?

· ·

☞   *the Supreme Court*

· ·

THE AUTHORITY OF the Supreme Court as the highest in the land originates from Article III of the Constitution. The Supreme Court is the ultimate arbiter of all cases and controversies in which there is a need to interpret the Constitution. When the Court agrees to hear a case, its sole intention is to examine and clarify a point of law, not to adjudicate guilt or innocence as in a criminal case. Judicial review enables the Court to invalidate both federal and state laws when they conflict with the Constitution. The decisions of the Court can be changed only by another Supreme Court decision or by a Constitutional amendment.

The Constitution gives the president the power to nominate Supreme Court justices, but all Supreme Court nominations must be confirmed by a majority vote in the Senate.

The framers of the Constitution wanted to ensure that members of the Supreme Court would be free

---

⭐ **EXEMPLARS OF GOOD JUDGMENT**

Match the justice with appropriate reference.

A. Authored an opinion in the landmark *case of Marbury v. Madison* (1803), which is considered the cornerstone of the principle of judicial review. It gives the Court the authority to invalidate any law that it finds to be unconstitutional.

B. The first Supreme Court justice to actually attend a law school.

C. Led the National Football League in rushing in 1938 as a running back for the Pittsburgh Pirates (now the Steelers).

D. Introduced the tradition of the "conference handshake." Before they take their seats at the bench, each justice shakes hands with the others. This jurist cited the practice as a way to remind the justices that, although they may have differences of opinion, they share a common purpose.

E. Appointed the first African American attorney to argue cases before the

1. Melville W. Fuller (1888–1910)
2. Thurgood Marshall (1967–91)
3. Warren Burger (1969–86)
4. Levi Woodbury (1845–51)
5. John Marshall (1801–35)
6. Byron R. White (1962–93)
7. Edward D. White (1894–1921)
8. Salmon P. Chase (1864–73)

from political pressure, so the Constitution provides that, once appointed, justices may remain in office "during good behavior" until they die or choose to retire. Their independence is further protected by a constitutional guarantee that their salaries will not be diminished (they can be increased) while they are in office.

Supreme Court and presided at the impeachment trial of President Andrew Johnson.

F. Nominated by Lyndon Baines Johnson, he was the first African American to become a Supreme Court justice. Prior to sitting on its bench, he represented and won more cases before the Supreme Court than any other practitioner.

G. Named chief justice by President Richard Nixon, he spoke for a unanimous Court (*United States v. Nixon, 1974*) upholding a subpoena for the Watergate tapes, which led to the president's resignation.

H. He fought on the Confederate side in the Civil War. The only person promoted to chief justice by the man who would succeed him, President William Howard Taft. Taft, in turn, is the only person to have been both president of the United States and chief justice of the United States.

39 How many justices are on the Supreme Court?

☞ *nine (9)*

GEORGE WASHINGTON SET a high standard when he nominated justices "with a sole view to the public good" and to "bring forward those who, upon every consideration and from the best information I can obtain, will in my judgment be most likely to answer that great end." Washington named only men he knew well, and he measured them against specific criteria, including the fitness of their character and health, rigorous training, and public recognition.

The first Supreme Court had six members and there have been as many as ten seats on the bench. Although it falls to Congress to legislate the number of judges on the High Court, President Franklin D. Roosevelt, in an effort to bolster his New Deal programs, supported "Court-packing" legislation to increase the number of justices on the Court.

40 Who is the chief justice of the United States?

☞ *John Roberts (John G. Roberts Jr.)*

JOHN G. ROBERTS JR. is the fifteenth chief justice of the United States. Nominated by President George W. Bush to take the seat of retiring justice Sandra Day O'Connor, his nomination was quickly changed to fill the position of chief justice when the incumbent, William H. Rehnquist, died in September 2005.

The chief justice of the United States is the head of the judicial branch of the government of the United States and presides over the Supreme Court. The chief justice also officiates at the inauguration of the president of the United States and presides when the Senate tries impeachments of the president.

The associate justices are Anthony M. Kennedy (1988), Clarence Thomas (1991), Ruth Bader Ginsburg (1993), Stephen G. Breyer (1994), Samuel Anthony Alito Jr. (2006), Sonia Sotomayor (2009), Elena Kagan (2010), and Neil M. Gorsuch (2017).

In the Court the justices are seated by seniority, with the chief justice in the center, the senior associate justice to the chief's right, the second senior to the chief's left, and so on, alternating right and left.

41 **Under our Constitution, some powers belong to the federal government. What is one power of the federal government?**

....

☞ *to print money, to declare war, to create an army, to make treaties*

....

42 **Under our Constitution, some powers belong to the states. What is one power of the states?**

☞ provide schooling and education, provide protection (police), provide safety (fire departments), give a driver's license, approve zoning
and land use

43 Who is the governor of your state?

☞ *Answers will vary. [Residents of the District of
Columbia and U.S. territories without a governor should say "we don't have a governor."]
Please see Appendix D, page 117 for the complete list of current U.S. governors.*

44 What is the capital of your state?

☞ *Answers will vary. [District of Columbia residents should answer that D.C. is not a state
and does not have a capital. Residents of U.S.
territories should name the capital of the territory.] Please see Appendix E, page 120.*

45 What are the two major political parties in the United States?

• •

☞ *Democratic and Republican*

• •

46 What is the political party of the president now?

• •

☞ ~~Republican (Party)~~ Democratic

• •

THE DEMOCRATIC PARTY traces its origin to the Democratic-Republican Party founded by Thomas Jefferson. The "modern" Democratic Party was formed from a faction of the Democratic-Republicans, led by Andrew Jackson.

The modern Republican Party traces its origins to a coalition formed from the Whig Party, the Know-Nothing Party, and the Free-Soil Party in opposition to the Kansas-Nebraska Act. Its first nominee for president of the United States, in 1856, was John C. Frémont. Its second nominee, in 1860, was Abraham Lincoln.

47 What is the name of the Speaker of the House of Representatives now?

35

☞ *Paul D. Ryan* ~~Paul D. Ryan~~
(Paul) Ryan Nancy Pelosi

THE SPEAKER OF the House is the presiding officer of the U.S. House of Representatives and is traditionally the head of the majority party in the House. He or she chairs the majority party's House steering committee and is responsible for ensuring that the House passes legislation supported by that party. The Speaker is second in the United States presidential line of succession, after the vice president.

RIGHTS AND RESPONSIBILITIES

48 **There are four amendments to the Constitution about who can vote. Describe one of them.**

☞ *Citizens eighteen (18) and older can vote; you don't have to pay (a poll tax) to vote; any citizen can vote (women and men can vote); a male citizen of any race can vote.*

49 **What is one responsibility that is only for United States citizens?**

☞ *serve on a jury, vote in a federal election*

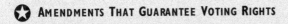

⭐ AMENDMENTS THAT GUARANTEE VOTING RIGHTS

FIFTEENTH AMENDMENT
Ratified February 3, 1870

Section 1

The right of citizens of the United States to vote shall not be denied or abridged by the United States or by any State on account of race, color, or previous condition of servitude.

NINETEENTH AMENDMENT
Ratified August 18, 1920

The right of citizens of the United States to vote shall not be denied or abridged by the United States or by any State on account of sex.

Let each citizen remember at the moment he is offering his vote that he is not making a present or a compliment to please an individual—or at least that he ought not so to do; but that he is executing one of the most solemn trusts in human society for which he is accountable to God and his country.

—Samuel Adams

TWENTY-FOURTH AMENDMENT
Ratified January 23, 1964

Section 1

The right of citizens of the United States to vote in any primary or other election for President or Vice President, for electors for President or Vice President, or for Senator or Representative in Congress, shall not be denied or abridged by the United States or any State by reason of failure to pay poll tax or other tax.

A share in the sovereignty of the state, which is exercised by the citizens at large, in voting at elections is one of the most important rights of the subject, and in a republic ought to stand foremost in the estimation of the law."

—Alexander Hamilton

TWENTY-SIXTH AMENDMENT
Ratified July 1, 1971

Section 1

The right of citizens of the United States, who are eighteen years of age or older, to vote shall not be denied or abridged by the United States or by any State on account of age.

To make democracy work, we must be a nation of participants, not simply observers. One who does not vote has no right to complain.

—Louis L'Amour

50 What are two rights only for United States citizens?

☞ *apply for a federal job, vote, run for federal office, carry a U.S. passport, serve on a jury*

51 What are two rights of everyone living in the United States?

☞ *freedom of expression   freedom to petition freedom of assembly   the government*

freedom of worship   *the right to bear arms*
freedom of speech

. . . .

52   **What do we show loyalty to when we say the Pledge of Allegiance?**

. . . .

☞   *the United States, the flag*

. . . .

53   **What is one promise you make when you become a United States citizen?**

. . . .

☞   *give up loyalty to other countries*
defend the Constitution and laws of the
    United States
obey the laws of the United States
serve in the U.S. military (if needed)
serve (do important work for) the nation (if
    needed)
be loyal to the United States

. . . .

⭐ Martin Van Buren was the first president to be born a U.S. citizen. Presidents George Washington, John Adams, Thomas Jefferson, James Madison, James Monroe, John Quincy Adams, Andrew Jackson, and William Henry Harrison were born as British subjects before the United States was a country.

54 How old do citizens have to be to vote for president?

....

☞ *eighteen (18) and older*

....

55 What are two ways that Americans can participate in their democracy?

....

☞ *vote*
   help with a campaign
   join a community group
   call senators and representatives
   run for office

⭐ A man's country is not a certain area of land, of mountains, rivers, and woods, but it is a principle; and patriotism is loyalty to that principle.
—George William Curtis

May the sun in his course visit no land more free, more happy, more lovely, than this our own country!
—Daniel Webster

If our country is worth dying for in time of war let us resolve that it is truly worth living for in time of peace.
—Hamilton Fish

This country will not be a good place for any of us to live in unless we make it a good place for all of us to live in.
—Theodore Roosevelt

join a political party
join a civic group
give an elected official your opinion on an
  issue
publicly support or oppose an issue or policy
write to a newspaper

. . . .

56 When is the last day you can send in federal income tax forms?

. . . .

☞ *April 15*

. . . .

57 When must all men register for the Selective Service?

. . . .

☞ *at age eighteen (18), between eighteen (18)
and twenty-six (26)*

. . . .

AMERICAN HISTORY

. . . .

COLONIAL PERIOD AND INDEPENDENCE

58 What is one reason colonists came to America?

. . . .

☞ *freedom*   *political liberty*
  religious freedom   *economic opportunity*
  practice their religion *escape persecution*

. . . .

AMONG THOSE WHOSE ancestry can be traced to passengers on the *Mayflower* are Alec Baldwin, Humphrey Bogart, Bing Crosby, Clint Eastwood, Ralph Waldo Emerson, Hugh Hefner, Marilyn Monroe, Sarah Palin, Dan Quayle, Christopher Reeve, Alan B. Shepherd Jr., Joseph Smith, Noah Webster, Orson Welles, presidents John Adams, John Quincy Adams, James Garfield, Ulysses S. Grant, Franklin D. Roosevelt, and Zachary Taylor.

Want to see if your family tree has roots within the timbers of the Mayflower? Visit http://www.plymouth ancestors.org and the General Society of Mayflower Descendants' Web site at http://www.themayflower society.com.

59 Who lived in America before the Europeans arrived?

☞ *Native Americans, American Indians*

60 What group of people was taken to America and sold as slaves?

☞ *Africans, people from Africa*

61 Why did the colonists fight the British?

☞ *because of high taxes (taxation without representation), because the British army stayed in their houses (boarding, quartering), because they didn't have self-government*

THE FIRST CASUALTY associated with the American Revolutionary War was that of a black man named Crispus Attucks. He was among the five men who died during, or as a result of, the Boston Massacre on March 5, 1770. A color print of that night's events, titled The Bloody Massacre Perpetrated in King Street, which circulated a few weeks later, was a key document in encouraging anti-English sentiment. The artist-engraver of this now iconic print was a Boston artisan named Paul Revere.

The rebellious colonists did not move inexorably toward an all-out war with the Crown, from the battles of Lexington and Concord and the mobilization of more than thirteen thousand militia in April 1775 to the major engagement at the Battle of Bunker (Breeds) Hill. However, on July 5, 1775, the Continental Congress actually adopted the Olive Branch Petition, appealing directly to King George III for reconciliation. His Majesty refused to look at the petition and further pushed the colonists away by issuing a proclamation declaring the Americans to be in a state of open rebellion.

Although the American Revolution was a popular cause, not all colonials supported a break with England. Approximately five hundred thousand whites (20 percent of that population) were loyalists, or "Tories," who did not necessarily agree with British policies, such as the Stamp Act, but felt that peaceful means were the appropriate remedy.

The first major American victory in the Revolutionary War came on October 7, 1777 (fifteen months after the Declaration of Independence), at the Battle of Saratoga, New York. Ten days later General John Burgoyne and his army of fifty-seven hundred men surren-

 The hour is fast approaching, on which the Honor and Success of this army, and the safety of our bleeding Country depend. Remember, officers and Soldiers, that you are free men, fighting for the blessings of Liberty—that slavery will be your portion, and that of your posterity, if you do not acquit yourselves like men.

—George Washington, general orders, August 23, 1776

dered to the Americans led by General Horatio Gates. The British prisoners were marched to Boston, placed on ships, and sent back to England after swearing not to serve again in the war. News of the American victory at Saratoga traveled to Europe, after which Benjamin Franklin was received by the French Royal Court.

The French played a decisive role in the colonists' ability to defeat the British. In February 1778, America and France signed a Treaty of Amity and Commerce, in which France recognized America and offered trade concessions. The two nations also entered into a Treaty of Alliance, which stipulated that if France entered the war, neither country would lay down its arms until America won its independence, that neither would conclude peace with Britain without the consent of the other, and that each guaranteed the other's possessions in America.

The American Revolution effectively ended with the surrender of the British under Lord Cornwallis at Yorktown, Virginia, on October 19, 1781. However, British troops continued to hold New York City for two more years until they finally departed on November 25, 1783.

62 Who wrote the Declaration of Independence?

. . . .

☞ *(Thomas) Jefferson*

. . . .

IN MAY 1775, after the clashes at Lexington and Concord, Massachusetts, the Second Continental Congress, made up of delegates from twelve colonies (Georgia's delegation arrived in the autumn), convened in Philadelphia. Among its other duties, a committee was empaneled to draft a Declaration of Independence from Great Britain. Thomas Jefferson, who was perceived to have a "masterly pen," was asked to draft the initial version of the document. His rough draft of the declaration, with emendations by John Adams and Benjamin Franklin, is the document that was adopted by the Continental Congress; printed by John Dunlap, official printer to the Congress; and is in the safekeeping of the manuscript division of the Library of Congress. There are twenty-five known copies of the Dunlap-printed version.

Jefferson was initially reluctant to assume the position of author of the declaration, believing that fellow committee member John Adams was better qualified. But Adams convinced him otherwise, saying, "Reason first: You are a Virginian, and Virginia ought to appear at the head of this business. Reason second: I am obnoxious, suspected and unpopular; you are very much otherwise. Reason third: You can write 10 times better than I can."

The political philosophy of the declaration was not new: It drew key ideas and ideals from the works of British political philosopher John Locke, Continental philosophers, and the Virginia Declaration of Rights, but Jefferson's writing encapsulated these ideas into "self-evident truths" and set down a list of grievances against the king in order to justify to the world the breaking of ties between the colonies and Great Britain.

Jefferson's original draft included a denunciation of the slave trade, which was later edited out by the Continental Congress. (Ironically, Jefferson himself was a slaveowner.) John Adams, writing to Timothy Pickering in 1822, speculated: "I have long wondered that the original draft had not been published. I suppose the reason is the vehement philippic against Negro slavery."

63   When was the Declaration of Independence adopted?

☞   *July 4, 1776*

ON MAY 15, 1776, the Virginia Convention passed a resolution that "the delegates appointed to represent this colony in General Congress be instructed to propose to that respectable body to declare the United Colonies free and independent states." It was in the spirit of that directive that on June 7, 1776, Richard Henry Lee, a delegate from Virginia, introduced a resolution before the Continental Congress "that these United Colonies are, and of right ought to be, free and independent States, that they are absolved from all allegiance to the British Crown, and that all political connection between them and the State of Great Britain is, and ought to be, totally dissolved."

On June 11, 1776, Thomas Jefferson, John Adams, Benjamin Franklin, Roger Sherman, and Robert Livingston, known collectively as the Committee of Five, were appointed to draft a statement, incorporating the resolution in presenting the colonies' case for independence.

On July 2, 1776, the declaration with the Lee resolution was adopted by twelve of the thirteen colonies (New York did not vote in favor of it until July 9). Con-

⭐ Match the July 4 event with the year.

A. The death of John Adams and Thomas Jefferson on the fiftieth anniversary of the Declaration of Independence.

B. President Lyndon B. Johnson signed the Freedom of Information Act.

C. The beginning of construction for the Erie Canal.

D. The cornerstone of the Freedom Tower is laid on the World Trade Center site.

E. The opening of the U.S. Military Academy at West Point, New York.

F. The announcement of the Louisiana Purchase.

G. President Harry S. Truman's declaration of independence for the Philippines.

H. The debut of the fifty-star flag in Philadelphia.

I. The Statue of Liberty was presented to the U.S. in Paris.

J. The laying of the cornerstone of the Washington Monument.

1. 1802
2. 1803
3. 1817
4. 1826
5. 1960
6. 1850
7. 2004
8. 1884
9. 1946
10. 1966

ANSWERS: A-4, B-10, C-3, D-7, E-1, F-2, G-9, H-5, I-8, J-6

gress made some revisions to it on July 2 and 3, and on the morning of July 4. Although no one actually signed the Declaration of Independence on the afternoon of July 4, it was officially adopted that day, and the Committee of Five took the manuscript copy of the document to John Dunlap, official printer to the Congress.

On the morning of July 5, the printed copies were sent by Congress to various committees and assemblies and to the commanders of the Continental troops.

The first celebration of independence took place in Philadelphia with the ringing of the Liberty Bell, a parade, and the discharging of cannons on July 8, 1776.

July 4, Independence Day, was declared a federal holiday by Congress in 1941, during World War II.

64 There were thirteen original states. Name three.

· ·

☞ *New Hampshire*   *Massachusetts*
Rhode Island   *Connecticut*
New York   *New Jersey*
Pennsylvania   *Delaware*
Maryland   *Virginia*
North Carolina   *South Carolina*
Georgia

· ·

65 What happened at the Constitutional Convention?

· ·

☞ *The Constitution was written; the Founding Fathers wrote the Constitution.*

· ·

66 When was the Constitution written?

· ·

☞ *1787*

· ·

⭐ THE 13 ORIGINAL COLONIES/STATES

COLONY	YEAR FOUNDED	FOUNDED BY
Virginia	1607	London Company
Massachusetts	1620	Massachusetts Bay Company
Maryland	1634	Lord Baltimore
Connecticut	c. 1635	Thomas Hooker
Rhode Island	1636	Roger Williams
Delaware	1638	Peter Minuit and the New Sweden Company
New Hampshire	1638	John Wheelwright
North Carolina	1653	Virginians
South Carolina	1663	Eight nobles with a royal charter from Charles II
New Jersey	1664	Lord Berkeley and Sir George Carteret
New York	1664	Duke of York
Pennsylvania	1681	William Penn
Georgia	1732	James Edward Oglethorpe

GEORGE CLYMER, BENJAMIN Franklin, Robert Morris, George Read, Roger Sherman, and James Wilson signed both the Declaration of Independence and the Constitution. Roger Sherman was the only man to sign the Articles of Association, the Declaration of Independence, the Articles of Confederation, and the U.S. Constitution.

The first meeting of the Constitutional Convention, which was convened to revise the Articles of Confederation, took place in Philadelphia, the nation's largest and most diverse city at that time, in May 1787. Rhode

Island was the only state that did not send a delegate. During the course of the convention, it became clear that the articles could not be revised in a satisfactory manner, and the creation of a new constitution, with a stronger central government, was undertaken.

The Constitution became binding by the ratification of the ninth state, New Hampshire, on June 21, 1788. On March 3, 1789, the old Confederation of States went out of existence, and on March 4 the new government of the United States began legally to function. On April 6, the organizing of Congress—the legislative branch of the national government—began. On April 30, 1789, George Washington was inaugurated as president of the United States, making the executive branch of the government operative. On February 2, 1790, the Supreme Court, the head of the judicial branch, organized and held its first session, marking the date when our government became fully operative.

67 The *Federalist Papers* supported the passage of the U.S. Constitution. Name one of the writers.

. . . .

☞ *(James) Madison, (Alexander) Hamilton, (John) Jay, Publius*

. . . .

THE CONSTITUTION WAS sent to the states for ratification in September 1787. Alexander Hamilton, James Madison, and John Jay wrote the *Federalist Papers* under the pseudonym "Publius" in order to influence the vote in favor of ratification. Seventy-seven of the eighty-five essays

⭐ Match the American firsts.

1. The first Secretary of the U.S. Treasury.
2. The first chief justice of the U.S. Supreme Court.
3. The first person born in America to English parents.
4. The first U.S. Postmaster General, also known as the "first American."
5. The first First Lady to reside at the White House (President's house).
6. The first vice president under President George Washington.
7. The city where the first fire department, zoo, and hospital were established.
8. The city where the "shot heard 'round the word" was fired in 1775.
9. The city where the first colony was established in 1607.
10. The city where the first presidential inauguration took place in 1789.

A. Abigail Adams
B. Jamestown, Virginia
C. Alexander Hamilton
D. John Jay
E. Virginia Dare
F. New York City
G. John Adams
H. Philadelphia, Pennsylvania
I. Lexington, Massachusetts
J. Benjamin Franklin

ANSWERS: 1-C, 2-D, 3-E, 4-J, 5-A, 6-G, 7-H, 8-I, 9-B, 10-F

were published serially in three newspapers in New York. The balance were included in a two-volume compilation published in 1788 entitled *The Federalist*.

In addition to the relevance of these writings during the process of ratification, they have been cited, subsequently, as providing insight into the intentions of the framers of the Constitution by federal judges, and on the occasion of the Emancipation Proclamation, in a letter from Alexander Hamilton's son John to President Lincoln.

68 What is one thing Benjamin Franklin is famous for?

. . . .

☞ *U.S. diplomat, oldest member of the Constitutional Convention, first Postmaster General of the United States, writer of* **Poor Richard's Almanac**, *started the first free libraries*

. . . .

69 Who is the "Father of Our Country"?

. . . .

☞ *(George) Washington*

. . . .

GEORGE WASHINGTON WAS born in Westmoreland County, Virginia, on February 22, 1732. He was a surveyor, a British officer in the French and Indian War (1754–60), a member of the House of Burgesses, and a member of both the First (1774) and the Second (1775) Continental Congresses. In 1774 Washington coauthored with George Mason the Fairfax County Resolves, which protested the British "Intolerable Acts"—legislation passed by the British to punish the colonies in the wake of the December 16, 1773, Boston Tea Party. During the Revolutionary War, he was named the commander in chief of the Continental Army, having been nominated for that post by John Adams, who believed Washington was the one man who could unify the northern and southern colonies in the struggle for independence.

Gouverneur Morris, in his eulogy of Washington on his death in 1799, remarked: "Born to high destinies, he was fashioned for them by the hand of nature. His form was noble—his port majestic. On his front were enthroned the virtues which exalt, and those which adorn the human character. So dignified his deportment, no man could approach him but with respect—none was great in his presence. You have all seen him, and you all have felt the reverence he inspired."

Washington demurred from leading a public fight against slavery because he believed it could tear the new nation apart. However, in 1786, he wrote to Robert Morris that "there is not a man living who wishes more sincerely than I do, to see a plan adopted for the abolition of slavery." Washington arranged for the slaves he owned to be freed after the death of his wife, and he left instructions for the continued care and education of some of his former slaves and their children.

70 Who was the first president?

· ·

☞ *(George) Washington*

· ·

FIRST IN WAR, first in peace, and first in the hearts of his countrymen, George Washington was made the first president of the United States in 1789 by a unanimous vote of the electors. He took the oath of office at Federal Hall in New York City, the nation's first capital and served two full four-year terms through 1797.

Washington had a clear sense that he, and his peers, were laying the cornerstone for the future. He wrote to James Madison: "As the first of every thing in our situation will serve to establish a precedent it is devoutly wished on my part, that these precedents may be fixed on true principles."

"I do solemnly swear (or affirm) that I will faithfully execute the Office of President of the United States, and will to the best of my ability, preserve, protect and defend the Constitution of the United States." This oath, taken by George Washington on April 30, 1789, has remained the same for more than two hundred years. His refusal to accept a crown and his willingness to peacefully relinquish the office after two terms established the precedents for limits on the power of the presidency.

THE 1800s

71 **What territory did the United States buy from France in 1803?**

☞ *the Louisiana Territory, Louisiana*

72 **Name one war fought by the United States in the 1800s.**

☞ *War of 1812, Mexican-American War, Civil War, Spanish-American War*

THE WAR OF 1812 was a conflict between the United

States and Britain. Generally accepted causes of the conflict were trade restrictions imposed by Britain against the United States designed to curtail the flow of American goods being provided to the French under Napoleon, who were at war with Britain, the United States' objection to what it perceived to be the forced recruitment of its citizens into the British Navy, and British support of the American Indian Nations in their efforts to resist American expansion in the northwestern United States.

The Mexican-American War was a conflict between Mexico and the United States between 1846 and 1848. The war was precipitated by the annexation of Texas by the United States in 1845. As a result of the Treaty of Guadalupe Hidalgo, parts of modern-day Colorado, Arizona, New Mexico, and Wyoming, as well as all of California, Nevada, and Utah were ceded to the United States.

The Spanish-American War was a conflict between Spain and the United States that took place between April and August 1898 over the issues of the liberation of Cuba. On December 10, 1898, the signing of the Treaty of Paris gave the United States control of Cuba, the Philippines, Puerto Rico, and Guam.

73 Name the U.S. war between the North and the South.

. . . .

☞ *the Civil War, the War between the States*

. . . .

THE AMERICAN CIVIL War (1861–65) (the War Between the States) saw combat between the Confederate States of America (eleven Southern slave states that had seceded from the United States) and the free states and the five border slave states in the North. The American Civil War led to the death of more than 620,000 soldiers and numerous civilian casualties, but ended slavery in the United States, restored the Union, and strengthened the role of the federal government.

74 Name one problem that led to the Civil War.

☞ *slavery, economic reasons, states' rights*

75 What was one important thing that Abraham Lincoln did?

☞ *freed the slaves (Emancipation Proclamation), saved (or preserved) the Union, led the United States during the Civil War*

76 What did the Emancipation Proclamation do?

☞ *freed the slaves, freed slaves in the Confederacy, freed slaves in the Confederate states, freed slaves in most Southern states*

ON SEPTEMBER 22, 1862, after the Union Army victory at Antietam, Maryland, President Lincoln issued a preliminary proclamation stating that on January 1, 1863, he would free all the slaves in those states still in rebellion. The decree left room for a plan of compensated emancipation.

President Lincoln signed the final draft of the Emancipation Proclamation on January 1, 1863. It applied only to states that had seceded from the Union, effectively leaving slavery intact in the loyal border states. "All persons held as slaves within any State or designated part of the State, the people whereof shall then be in rebellion against the United States, shall be then, thenceforward, and forever free." Since the states that this affected no longer considered themselves to be under the jurisdiction of President Lincoln, the freedom he promised ultimately depended on a military victory by the Union. This irony was not lost on Secretary of State William Seward, who said, "We show our sympathy with slavery by emancipating slaves where we cannot reach them and holding them in bondage where we can set them free."

The Emancipation Proclamation signaled the acceptance of black men into the Union Army and Navy. By the end of the Civil War almost two hundred thousand black soldiers and sailors had fought for the Union.

The official end of slavery in America was achieved by the ratification of the Thirteenth Amendment to the Constitution on December 18, 1865, which read in part (Section 1): "Neither slavery nor involuntary servitude, except as a punishment for crime whereof the party shall have been duly convicted, shall exist within the United States, or any place subject to their jurisdiction."

A manuscript of the final version of the Emancipation Proclamation in Lincoln's hand, owned by the Chicago Historical Society, was destroyed in that city's famous fire in 1871. A manuscript version of the Preliminary Emancipation Proclamation, owned by New York State, was saved from the same fate in a fire in Albany, New York, in 1911.

77 What did Susan B. Anthony do?

☞ *fought for women's rights, fought for civil rights*

RECENT AMERICAN HISTORY AND OTHER IMPORTANT HISTORICAL INFORMATION

78 Name one war fought by the United States in the 1900s.

☞ *World War I, World War II, Korean War, Vietnam War, (Persian) Gulf War*

79 Who was president during World War I?

☞ *(Woodrow) Wilson*

80 Who was president during the Great Depression and World War II?

☞ *(Franklin) Roosevelt*

81 Who did the United States fight in World War II?

☞ *Japan, Germany, and Italy*

82 Before he was president, Eisenhower was a general. What war was he in?

☞ *World War II*

83 During the Cold War, what was the main concern of the United States?

☞ *Communism*

84 What movement tried to end racial discrimination?

☞ civil rights (movement)

85 What did Martin Luther King Jr. do?

☞ fought for civil rights, worked for equality for all Americans

MARTIN LUTHER KING JR. was born Michael but later had his name changed in honor of the Protestant reformer Martin Luther.

The Reverend Dr. King was the president of the Montgomery (Alabama) Improvement Association, the organization that was responsible for the successful Montgomery Bus Boycott of 381 days during 1955 and 1956. On December 21, 1956, after the Supreme Court had declared unconstitutional the laws requiring segregation on buses, blacks and whites rode the buses as equals.

Between 1957 and 1968 Dr. King traveled more than six million miles and spoke some twenty-five hundred times, preaching nonviolent resistance in an effort to achieve civil rights and racial equality for African Americans and other people of color.

Dr. King was one of the leaders of the March on Washington for Jobs and Freedom on August 28, 1963, which was attended by approximately 250,000 people. The "I Have a Dream" speech he delivered in front of the Lincoln Memorial became a signal moment of the civil rights movement. He was named Man of the Year by *Time* magazine in 1963.

In 1964, at age thirty-five, Dr. King became the youngest man to receive the Nobel Peace Prize. He was the second American to be awarded the prestigious prize. The first was Dr. Ralph J. Bunche, also an African American, who received the prize in 1950 for his work as a United Nations mediator leading to the 1949 Arab-Israeli armistice agreement. Dr. King's ability to focus attention and mobilize public opinion was an important contributing factor in the passage by Congress of the Civil Rights Act of 1964, outlawing segregation in public accommodations and discrimination in education and employment, and the Voting Rights Act of 1965, which suspended (later banned) literacy tests and other restrictions that impeded African Americans and other minorities from voting. Dr. King was assassinated on April 4, 1968, in Memphis, Tennessee.

The campaign to establish a federal holiday in Dr. King's honor began soon after his assassination. President Reagan signed the holiday into law in 1983, and it was first observed in 1986. It was officially observed in all fifty states for the first time in 2000.

86   What major event happened on September 11, 2001, in the United States?

☞   *Terrorists attacked the United States.*

TERRORISTS AFFILIATED WITH al-Qaeda hijacked four commercial passenger jet airliners in a series of coordinated movements and intentionally crashed two of the airliners into the Twin Towers of the World Trade Center (WTC) in New York City.

All of the passengers and terrorists as well as thousands working in the buildings perished. The WTC towers collapsed, destroying nearby buildings and damaging others. The hijackers crashed a third airliner into the Pentagon in Washington, D.C. The fourth plane crashed into a field in rural Somerset County, Pennsylvania, after some of its passengers and flight crew attempted to retake control of the plane. There were no survivors from any of the flights.

87 Name one American Indian tribe in the United States.

☞
Cherokee	Navajo	Sioux
Chippewa	Choctaw	Pueblo
Apache	Iroquois	Creek
Blackfeet	Seminole	Cheyenne
Arawak	Shawnee	Mohegan
Huron	Oneida	Lakota
Crow	Teton	Hopi
Inuit		

INTEGRATED CIVICS

· ·

GEOGRAPHY

88 Name one of the two longest rivers in the United States.

· ·

☞ *Missouri (River), Mississippi (River)*

· ·

THE 2,540-MILE MISSOURI River flows through the states of Montana, North Dakota, South Dakota, Nebraska, Kansas, Iowa, and Missouri. The 2,320-mile long Mississippi River flows through the states of Minnesota, Wisconsin, Iowa, Illinois, Kentucky, Tennessee, Missouri, Arkansas, Mississippi, and Louisiana.

89 What ocean is on the West Coast of the United States?

· ·

☞ *Pacific (Ocean)*

· ·

THE 7,623-MILE GENERAL Pacific coastline runs along the states of California, Oregon, and Washington in the lower forty-eight, and off the mainland it provides coastline for Alaska and Hawaii.

90 What ocean is on the East Coast of the United States?

. . . .

☞　*Atlantic (Ocean)*

. . . .

THE 2,069-MILE GENERAL Atlantic coastline runs along the states of Maine, New Hampshire, Massachusetts, Rhode Island, Connecticut, New York, New Jersey, Delaware, Maryland, Virginia, North Carolina, South Carolina, Georgia, and Florida.

91 Name one U.S. territory.

. . . .

☞　*Puerto Rico, U.S. Virgin Islands, American Samoa, Northern Mariana Islands, Guam*

. . . .

92 Name one state that borders Canada.

. . . .

☞　
Maine	*New Hampshire*	*Vermont*
New York	*Pennsylvania*	*Ohio*
Michigan	*Minnesota*	*North Dakota*
Montana	*Idaho*	*Washington*
Alaska		

. . . .

THE BORDER BETWEEN Canada and the United States, officially known as the International Boundary, is not militarized, a fact made even more remarkable because these two nations share more than 5,500 miles of border, the longest common border in the world. The United States borders the Canadian provinces of New Brunswick, Quebec, Ontario, Manitoba, Saskatchewan, Alberta, British Columbia, and the Yukon Territory.

93 Name one state that borders Mexico.

. . . .

☞ *California, Arizona, New Mexico, Texas*

. . . .

THE 1,969-MILE BORDER between the United States and Mexico is reported to be the most frequently crossed border in the world. The United States borders the Mexican states of Baja California, Sonora, Chihuahua, Coahuila, Nuevo León, and Tamaulipas.

94 What is the capital of the United States?

. . . .

☞ *Washington, D.C.*

. . . .

IN DECEMBER 1790, George Washington signed the Residency Act, which declared that the federal government would reside in a district "not exceeding 10 miles square . . . on the river Potomac." On December 1,

1800, the federal capital was transferred from Philadelphia to that site, now called the city of Washington, in the territory of Columbia (so named in honor of Christopher Columbus). It is not part of any state but is a unique, federally managed district within the United States that is allowed to exercise limited local rule.

The overall design of this planned city was the work of Pierre Charles L'Enfant, an architect and city planner who was a military engineer with Major General Lafayette during the American Revolutionary War. The nation's capital houses the three branches of the federal government; the Smithsonian Institution (our national museum); memorials dedicated to George Washington, Thomas Jefferson, Abraham Lincoln, Franklin Delano Roosevelt, the veterans of WWII, the Korean conflict, and the war in Vietnam.

The land that became the District of Columbia was ceded by two slave states, Maryland and Virginia. Sadly, the majority of the labor force used to build the White House and the U.S. Capitol were African American slaves. Congress abolished slavery in the federal district on April 16, 1862, predating the Emancipation Proclamation and the adoption of the Thirteenth Amendment to the Constitution.

95   Where is the Statue of Liberty?

. . . .

☞   *New York (Harbor), Liberty Island (Also acceptable are New Jersey, near New York City, and on the Hudson River.)*

. . . .

⭐ The poem "The New Colossus" was written by Emma Lazarus in 1883 to help fund-raising for the pedestal of the statue. A bronze plaque inscribed with the poem was placed inside of the statue in 1903.

> Not like the brazen giant of Greek fame,
> With conquering limbs astride from land to land;
> Here at our sea-washed, sunset gates shall stand
> A mighty woman with a torch, whose flame
> Is the imprisoned lightning, and her name
> Mother of Exiles. From her beacon-hand
> Glows world-wide welcome; her mild eyes command
> The air-bridged harbor that twin cities frame,
> "Keep, ancient lands, your storied pomp!" cries she
> With silent lips. "Give me your tired, your poor,
> Your huddled masses yearning to breathe free,
> The wretched refuse of your teeming shore,
> Send these, the homeless, tempest-tost to me,
> I lift my lamp beside the golden door!"

THE STATUE, ALSO known as Lady Liberty, has become a universal symbol of freedom and hope. She welcomed arriving immigrants, who could see the statue as they arrived in the United States on the Atlantic side. The Statue of Liberty was presented to the United States by the people of France in 1886 to commemorate the centennial of the signing of the United States Declaration of Independence.

In 1984, the United Nations designated the Statue of Liberty as a World Heritage Site.

96 Why does the flag have thirteen stripes?

∙∙

☞ *because there were thirteen original colonies, because the stripes represent the original colonies*

∙∙

ON JUNE 14, 1777, the Continental Congress passed the first Flag Act: "Resolved, That the flag of the United States be made of thirteen stripes, alternate red and white; that the union be thirteen stars, white in a blue field, representing a new Constellation." George Washington (1789–94) was the only president to serve under this initial version of the flag.

The lovely story about Betsy Ross is just that—a story. As we learned, General Washington, accompanied by two members of Congress, visited Mrs. Ross in her home and asked that she create a flag from a drawing that they had brought. At her suggestion, General Washington made revisions in the design. When they returned, she presented them with the completed Stars and Stripes. However, this version of the story, never borne out by historical evidence, was first published by a grandson of Mrs. Ross in 1870, more than ninety years after the "fact."

Francis Hopkinson, a signer of the Declaration of Independence, lawyer, congressman from New Jersey, poet, artist, and civil servant with a distinguished career (according to the journals of the Continental Congress), is a good candidate as the designer of the first Stars and Stripes. Payment for his work (which he ultimately failed to receive due to an odd series of events concerning his actual role in the design, and political enmity) was to be a "quarter cask of the public wine."

The fifteen-star, fifteen-stripe flag, adding two stripes and two stars for the new states of Vermont and Kentucky was the only U.S. flag to have more than thirteen stripes. It survived the bombardment of Fort McHenry during the War of 1812, when Francis Scott Key wrote the poem that became the lyrics for "The Star-Spangled Banner." The flag act of April 4, 1818, provided for a return to the thirteen-stripe design and designated that one star symbolize each state, a new one to be added to the flag on the Fourth of July following the admission of each new state.

On June 24, 1912, President William Howard Taft established the official proportions of the elements of the flag and provided for arrangement of the stars in six horizontal rows of eight each to accommodate the statehood of New Mexico and Arizona, as the forty-seventh and forty-eighth states, a single point of each star to be facing upward.

The U.S. Army and Navy have a traditional way of folding the flag into the shape of a three-cornered hat, emblematic of the hats worn by colonial soldiers during the war for independence. The red and white stripes are folded under so that all that can be seen is a triangle of blue with several stars. When a flag is so worn out that it is no longer fit to serve as a symbol of our country, it should be destroyed by burning in a dignified manner. Many American Legion posts regularly conduct such a ceremony, often on Flag Day, June 14.

97   Why does the flag have fifty stars?

☞   *because there is one star for each state, because each star represents a state, because there are fifty states*

BY AN EXECUTIVE order of President Eisenhower, on January 3, 1959, a forty-ninth star was added to the flag in honor of the statehood of Alaska, and another executive order on August 21, 1959, provided for a fiftieth star to celebrate the statehood of Hawaii.

98   What is the name of the national anthem?

☞   *"The Star-Spangled Banner"*

DURING THE WAR of 1812, Francis Scott Key and Colonel John Skinner, the government's prisoner of war exchange agent, were sent to negotiate the release of a prisoner named Dr. William Beanes from the British. Key and Skinner unwittingly boarded a British warship in Chesapeake Bay as it was preparing to bombard Fort McHenry in Baltimore. The British agreed to release Dr. Beanes but continued to hold all three Americans until the battle was over. The bombardment began on September 13, 1814, and continued through the night. Key's morning view was obscured by the smoky haze lingering in the aftermath of the battle. At 7:00 a.m., a thinning mist showed that the American flag was still flying over the fort. An ecstatic Key wrote the verses to "The Star-Spangled Banner" and soon thereafter had it published as the "Defense of Fort McHenry."

His poem attained wide popularity set to the tune of a British drinking song "To Anacreon in Heaven," which we now know as "The Star-Spangled Banner." The song that we are accustomed to singing as "The Star-Spangled Banner" is actually only the first of four verses of the text. Key actually wrote:

> Oh, say can you see, by the dawn's early light,
> What so proudly we hailed at the twilight's last gleaming?
> Whose broad stripes and bright stars, through the perilous fight,
> O'er the ramparts we watched, were so gallantly streaming?
> And the rockets' red glare, the bombs bursting in air,
> Gave proof through the night that our flag was still there.
> Oh say, does that star-spangled banner yet wave
> O'er the land of the free and the home of the brave?
>
> On the shore, dimly seen through the mists of the deep,
> Where the foe's haughty host in dread silence reposes,
> What is that which the breeze, o'er the towering steep,
> As it fitfully blows, now conceals, now discloses?
> Now it catches the gleam of the morning's first beam,
> In full glory reflected now shines on the stream:
> 'Tis the star-spangled banner! O long may it wave
> O'er the land of the free and the home of the brave.
>
> And where is that band who so vauntingly swore
> That the havoc of war and the battle's confusion
> A home and a country should leave us no more?

Their blood has wiped out their foul footstep's pollution.
No refuge could save the hireling and slave
From the terror of flight, or the gloom of the grave: And
    the star-spangled banner in triumph doth wave
O'er the land of the free and the home of the brave.

Oh! thus be it ever, when freemen shall stand
Between their loved homes and the war's desolation!
Blest with victory and peace, may the heaven-rescued land
Praise the Power that hath made and preserved us a nation.
Then conquer we must, for our cause it is just,
And this be our motto: "In God is our trust."
And the star-spangled banner forever shall wave
O'er the land of the free and the home of the brave!

HOLIDAYS

99 **When do we celebrate Independence Day?**

. . . .

☞ *July 4*

. . . .

100 **Name two national U.S. holidays.**

. . . .

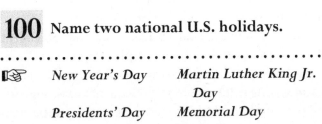

☞ *New Year's Day*   *Martin Luther King Jr.*
                                      Day

 Presidents' Day   *Memorial Day*

· ·

PRESIDENTS' DAY ORIGINALLY celebrated George Washington's birthday and is a United States federal holiday celebrated on the third Monday of February.

Formerly known as Decoration Day, Memorial Day, celebrated on the last Monday of May, commemorates the men and women who died while in military service to our country. First enacted to honor the Union dead of the American Civil War, it was expanded after World War I to include American casualties of any war or military action.

Labor Day is a federal holiday observed on the first Monday in September. The holiday originated in 1882 as a day off for the "working citizens." Congress made Labor Day a federal holiday in 1894, two months after the May Day Riots of 1894.

Columbus Day, celebrated on October 21, marks the anniversary of Christopher Columbus's arrival in the Americas.

Veterans Day is a federal holiday honoring military veterans, usually observed on November 11. It is also celebrated as Armistice Day or Remembrance Day in other parts of the world, the anniversary of the signing of the armistice that ended World War I.

The first New England Thanksgiving, the antecedent of our current celebration, took place in 1621 at Plymouth, Massachusetts. There are conflicting allusions to Thanksgiving celebrations in subsequent years, suggesting that similar occasions were celebrated but perhaps not on a regular basis or on a set date. As commander in chief of the Continental forces, George Washington issued a general order setting aside December 18, 1777, as a day "for Solemn Thanksgiving and Praise." As president he proclaimed Thursday, November 26, 1789, as the first national day of Thanksgiving.

Thanksgiving was celebrated on the last Thursday of November until 1939, when President Franklin D. Roosevelt moved it one week earlier. He was responding to pressure from the National Retail Dry Goods Association to aid business by lengthening the shopping period before Christmas. In 1941 Congress passed legislation that the fourth Thursday of November would be observed as a federal holiday beginning in 1942.

Order of Presidential Succession

Vice President
Speaker of the House
President pro tempore of the Senate
Secretary of State
Secretary of the Treasury
Secretary of Defense
Attorney General
Secretary of the Interior
Secretary of Agriculture
Secretary of Commerce
Secretary of Labor
Secretary of Health & Human Services
Secretary of Housing & Urban Development
Secretary of Transportation
Secretary of Energy
Secretary of Education
Secretary of Veterans Affairs
Secretary of Homeland Security

APPENDIX A

At a Glance: The USCIS Questions and Answers for the Naturalization Test*

. . . .

AMERICAN GOVERNMENT
Principles of American Democracy

1 What is the supreme law of the land?

. . . .

☞ *The Constitution*

. . . .

2 What does the Constitution do?

. . . .

☞ *sets up the government*
defines the government
protects basic rights of Americans

. . . .

---

* If you are 65 years old or older and have been a legal permanent resident of the United States for 20 or more years, you may study just the questions that have been marked with an asterisk.

3 The idea of self-government is in the first three words of the Constitution. What are these words?

☞ *We the People*

4 What is an amendment?

☞ *a change (to the Constitution)*
an addition (to the Constitution)

5 What do we call the first ten amendments to the Constitution?

☞ *The Bill of Rights*

6 What is one right or freedom from the First Amendment?*

☞ *speech*
religion
assembly
press
petition the government

7 How many amendments does the Constitution have?

☞ *twenty-seven (27)*

8 What did the Declaration of Independence do?

☞ *announced our independence (from Great Britain)*
declared our independence (from Great Britain)
said that the United States is free (from Great Britain)

9 What are two rights in the Declaration of Independence?

☞ *life*
liberty
pursuit of happiness

10 What is freedom of religion?

☞ *You can practice any religion, or not practice a religion.*

11 What is the economic system in the United States?*

☞ *capitalist economy*
market economy

12 What is the "rule of law"?

☞ *Everyone must follow the law.*
Leaders must obey the law.
Government must obey the law.
No one is above the law.

System of Government

13 Name one branch or part of the government.*

☞ *Congress*   *legislative*
president   *executive*
the courts   *judicial*

14 What stops one branch of government from becoming too powerful?

☞ *checks and balances*
separation of powers

15 **Who is in charge of the executive branch?**

☞ *the president*

16 **Who makes federal laws?**

☞ *Congress*
Senate and House (of Representatives)
(U.S. or national) legislature

17 **What are the two parts of the U.S. Congress?***

☞ *the Senate and House (of Representatives)*

18 **How many U.S. senators are there?**

☞ *one hundred (100)*

19 We elect a U.S. senator for how many years?

☞ *six (6)*

20 Who is one of your state's U.S. senators?*

☞ *Answers will vary. [For District of Columbia residents and residents of U.S. territories, the answer is that D.C. (or the territory where the applicant lives) has no U.S. Senators.]*

21 The House of Representatives has how many voting members?

☞ *four hundred thirty-five (435)*

22 We elect a U.S. Representative for how many years?

☞ *two (2)*

23 Name your U.S. representative.

☞ *Answers will vary. [Residents of territories with nonvoting delegates or resident commissioners may provide the name of that delegate or commissioner. Also acceptable is any statement that the territory has no (voting) representatives in Congress.]*

24 Whom does a U.S. senator represent?

☞ *all people of the state*

25 Why do some states have more representatives than other states?

☞ *(because of) the state's population*
(because) they have more people
(because) some states have more people

26 We elect a president for how many years?

☞ *four (4)*

27 In what month do we vote for president?*

☞ *November*

28 What is the name of the president of the United States now?*

☞ *Donald Trump*
Donald J. Trump
Trump

29 What is the name of the vice president of the United States now?

☞ *Mike Pence*
Michael Richard Pence
Pence

30 If the President can no longer serve, who becomes President?

☞ *the vice president*

31 If both the president and the vice president can no longer serve, who becomes president?

☞ *the Speaker of the House*

32 Who is the commander in chief of the military?

☞ *the president*

33 Who signs bills to become laws?

☞ *the president*

34 Who vetoes bills?

☞ *the president*

35   What does the president's cabinet do?

☞   *advises the president*

36   What are two cabinet-level positions?

☞   *Secretary of Agriculture*
Secretary of Commerce
Secretary of Defense
Secretary of Education
Secretary of Energy
Secretary of Health and Human Services
Secretary of Homeland Security
Secretary of Housing and Urban Development
Secretary of Interior
Secretary of State
Secretary of Transportation
Secretary of Treasury
Secretary of Veterans' Affairs
Secretary of Labor
Attorney General
Vice President

37   What does the judicial branch do?

☞   *reviews laws*
explains laws

resolves disputes (disagreements)
decides if a law goes against the Constitution

. . . .

38 What is the highest court in the United States?

. . . .

☞ *the Supreme Court*

. . . .

39 How many justices are on the Supreme Court?

. . . .

☞ *nine (9)*

. . . .

40 Who is the Chief Justice of the United States?

. . . .

☞ *John Roberts (John G. Roberts Jr.)*

. . . .

41 Under our Constitution, some powers belong to the federal government. What is one power of the federal government?

. . . .

☞ *to print money*
to declare war

to create an army
to make treaties

. . . .

42 **Under our Constitution, some powers belong to the states. What is one power of the states?**

. . . .

☞ *provide schooling and education*
provide protection (police)
provide safety (fire departments)
give a driver's license
approve zoning and land use

. . . .

43 **Who is the governor of your state?**

. . . .

☞ *Answers will vary. [Residents of the District of Columbia and U.S. territories without a governor should say "we don't have a governor."]*

. . . .

44 **What is the capital of your state?***

. . . .

☞ *Answers will vary. [District of Columbia residents should answer that D.C. is not a state and does not have a capital. Residents of U.S. territories should name the capital of the territory.]*

. . . .

45 What are the two major political parties in the United States?*

☞ *Democratic and Republican*

46 What is the political party of the President now?

☞ *Republican (Party)*

47 What is the name of the Speaker of the House of Representatives now?

☞ *Paul D. Ryan,*
(Paul) Ryan

Rights and Responsibilities

48 There are four amendments to the Constitution about who can vote. Describe one of them.

☞ *Citizens eighteen (18) and older (can vote).*
You don't have to pay (a poll tax) to vote.
Any citizen can vote. (Women and men can vote.)
A male citizen of any race (can vote).

49 What is one responsibility that is only for United States citizens?*

☞ serve on a jury
vote in a federal election

50 What are two rights only for United States citizens?

☞ apply for a federal job
vote
run for federal office
carry a U.S. passport

51 What are two rights of everyone living in the United States?

☞ freedom of expression
freedom of speech
freedom of assembly
freedom to petition the government
freedom of worship
the right to bear arms

52 What do we show loyalty to when we say the Pledge of Allegiance?

☞   *the United States*
      the flag

53   **What is one promise you make when you become a United States citizen?**

☞   *give up loyalty to other countries*
      defend the Constitution and laws of the
        United States
      obey the laws of the United States
      serve in the U.S. military (if needed)
      serve (do important work for) the nation (if
        needed)
      be loyal to the United States

54   **How old do citizens have to be to vote for president?***

☞   *eighteen (18) and older*

55   **What are two ways that Americans can participate in their democracy?**

☞   *vote*
      join a political party
      help with a campaign

join a civic group
join a community group
*give an elected official your opinion on an
    issue*
call senators and representatives
publicly support or oppose an issue or policy
run for office
write to a newspaper

. . . .

56 **When is the last day you can send in
federal income tax forms?***

. . . .

☞ *April 15*

. . . .

57 **When must all men register for the
Selective Service?**

. . . .

☞ *at age eighteen (18)*
between eighteen (18) and twenty-six (26)

. . . .

AMERICAN HISTORY
Colonial Period and Independence

58 **What is one reason colonists came to
America?**

☞ *freedom*
political liberty
religious freedom
economic opportunity
practice their religion
escape persecution

59 Who lived in America before the Europeans arrived?

☞ *Native Americans*
American Indians

60 What group of people was taken to America and sold as slaves?

☞ *Africans*
people from Africa

61 Why did the colonists fight the British?

☞ *because of high taxes (taxation without representation)*
because the British army stayed in their houses (boarding, quartering)
because they didn't have self-government

62 Who wrote the Declaration of Independence?

☞ *(Thomas) Jefferson*

63 When was the Declaration of Independence adopted?

☞ *July 4, 1776*

64 There were thirteen original states. Name three.

☞ *New Hampshire*   *Massachusetts*
Rhode Island   *Connecticut*
New York   *New Jersey*
Pennsylvania   *Delaware*
Maryland   *Virginia*
North Carolina   *South Carolina*
Georgia

65 What happened at the Constitutional Convention?

☞ *The Constitution was written.*
The Founding Fathers wrote the Constitution.

66 When was the Constitution written?

☞ *1787*

67 The *Federalist Papers* supported the passage of the U.S. Constitution. Name one of the writers.

☞ *(James) Madison*
(Alexander) Hamilton
(John) Jay
Publius

68 What is one thing Benjamin Franklin is famous for?

☞ *U.S. diplomat*
oldest member of the Constitutional Convention
first Postmaster General of the United States
writer of **Poor Richard's Almanac**
started the first free libraries

69 Who is the "Father of Our Country"?

☞ *(George) Washington*

70 Who was the first president?*

☞ *(George) Washington*

1800s

71 What territory did the United States buy from France in 1803?

☞ *the Louisiana Territory*
Louisiana

72 Name one war fought by the United States in the 1800s.

☞ *War of 1812*
Mexican-American War
Civil War
Spanish-American War

73 Name the U.S. war between the North and the South.

☞ *the Civil War*
the War between the States

74 Name one problem that led to the Civil War.

☞ *slavery*
economic reasons
states' rights

75 What was one important thing that Abraham Lincoln did?*

☞ *freed the slaves (Emancipation Proclamation)*
saved (or preserved) the Union
led the United States during the Civil War

76 What did the Emancipation Proclamation do?

☞ *freed the slaves*
freed slaves in the Confederacy
freed slaves in the Confederate states
freed slaves in most Southern states

77 What did Susan B. Anthony do?

☞ *fought for women's rights*
fought for civil rights

Recent American History and Other Important Historical Information

78 **Name one war fought by the United States in the 1900s.***

☞ *World War I*
World War II
Korean War
Vietnam War
(Persian) Gulf War

79 **Who was president during World War I?**

☞ *(Woodrow) Wilson*

80 **Who was president during the Great Depression and World War II?**

☞ *(Franklin) Roosevelt*

81 **Who did the United States fight in World War II?**

☞ *Japan, Germany, and Italy*

82 Before he was president, Eisenhower was a general. What war was he in?

☞ *World War II*

83 During the Cold War, what was the main concern of the United States?

☞ *Communism*

84 What movement tried to end racial discrimination?

☞ *civil rights (movement)*

85 What did Martin Luther King Jr. do?*

☞ *fought for civil rights*
worked for equality for all Americans

86 What major event happened on September 11, 2001, in the United States?

☞ *Terrorists attacked the United States.*

87 Name one American Indian tribe in the United States.

☞ *[Adjudicators will be supplied with a complete list.]*

Cherokee	*Navajo*
Sioux	*Chippewa*
Choctaw	*Pueblo*
Apache	*Iroquois*
Creek	*Blackfeet*
Seminole	*Cheyenne*
Arawak	*Shawnee*
Mohegan	*Huron*
Oneida	*Lakota*
Crow	*Teton*
Hopi	*Inuit*

INTEGRATED CIVICS
Geography

88 Name one of the two longest rivers in the United States.

☞ *Missouri (River)*
Mississippi (River)

89 What ocean is on the West Coast of the United States?

··

☞   *Pacific (Ocean)*

··

90 What ocean is on the East Coast of the United States?

··

☞   *Atlantic (Ocean)*

··

91 Name one U.S. territory.

··

☞   *Puerto Rico*
      U.S. Virgin Islands
      American Samoa
      Northern Mariana Islands
      Guam

··

92 Name one state that borders Canada.

··

☞   *Maine*   *New Hampshire*
      Vermont   *New York*
      Pennsylvania *Ohio*
      Michigan   *Minnesota*
      North Dakota *Montana*
      Idaho   *Washington*
      Alaska

··

93 Name one state that borders Mexico.

☞ California   Arizona
    New Mexico   Texas

94 What is the capital of the United States?*

☞ Washington, D.C.

95 Where is the Statue of Liberty?*

☞ New York (Harbor)
    Liberty Island
    [Also acceptable are New Jersey, near New York
    City, and on the Hudson (River).]

Symbols

96 Why does the flag have thirteen stripes?

☞   because there were thirteen original colonies
       because the stripes represent the original
          colonies

97 Why does the flag have fifty stars?*

☞   because there is one star for each state
       because each star represents a state
       because there are fifty states

98 What is the name of the national anthem?

☞   *"The Star-Spangled Banner"*

Holidays

99 When do we celebrate Independence Day?*

☞   *July 4*

100 Name two national U.S. holidays.

☞ *New Year's Day*
Martin Luther King Jr. Day
Presidents' Day
Memorial Day
Independence Day
Labor Day
Columbus Day
Veterans Day
Thanksgiving
Christmas

APPENDIX B

U.S. Senators
(as of January 20, 2017)

• •

For information on how to contact your senator, please visit http://www.senate.gov/senators/contact.

ALABAMA
• Shelby, Richard C. (R)
• Strange, Luther J. (R)

ALASKA
• Murkowski, Lisa (R)
• Sullivan, Dan (R)

ARIZONA
• Flake, Jeff (R)
• McCain, John (R)

ARKANSAS
• Boozman, John (R)
• Cotton, Tom (R)

CALIFORNIA
• Feinstein, Dianne (D)
• Harris, Kamala (D)

COLORADO
• Bennet, Michael F. (D)
• Gardner, Cory (R)

CONNECTICUT
• Blumenthal, Richard (D)
• Murphy, Christopher (D)

DELAWARE
• Carper, Thomas R. (D)
• Coons, Christopher (D)

FLORIDA
• Nelson, Bill (D)
• Rubio, Marco (R)

GEORGIA
• Isakson, Johnny (R)
• Perdue, David (R)

HAWAII
• Hirono, Mazie (D)
• Schatz, Brian (D)

IDAHO
• Crapo, Mike (R)
• Risch, James E. (R)

ILLINOIS
- Duckworth, Tammy (D)
- Durbin, Richard (D)

INDIANA
- Donnelly, Joe (D)
- Young, Todd (R)

IOWA
- Ernst, Joni (R)
- Grassley, Chuck (R)

KANSAS
- Moran, Jerry (R)
- Roberts, Pat (R)

KENTUCKY
- McConnell, Mitch (R)
- Paul, Rand (R)

LOUISIANA
- Cassidy, Bill (R)
- Kennedy, John N. (R)

MAINE
- Collins, Susan M. (R)
- King, Angus, Jr. (I)

MARYLAND
- Cardin, Benjamin L. (D)
- Van Hollen, Chris (D)

MASSACHUSETTS
- Markey, Ed (D)
- Warren, Elizabeth (D)

MICHIGAN
- Peters, Gary (D)
- Stabenow, Debbie (D)

MINNESOTA
- Franken, Al (D)
- Klobuchar, Amy (D)

MISSISSIPPI
- Cochran, Thad (R)
- Wicker, Roger F. (R)

MISSOURI
- Blunt, Roy (R)
- McCaskill, Claire (D)

MONTANA
- Daines, Steve (R)
- Tester, Jon (D)

NEBRASKA
- Fischer, Deb (R)
- Sasse, Ben (R)

NEVADA
- Cortez Masto, Catherine (D)
- Heller, Dean (R)

NEW HAMPSHIRE
- Hassan, Maggie (D)
- Shaheen, Jeanne (D)

NEW JERSEY
- Booker, Cory (D)
- Menendez, Robert (D)

NEW MEXICO
- Heinrich, Martin (D)
- Udall, Tom (D)

NEW YORK
- Gillibrand, Kirsten E. (D)
- Schumer, Charles E. (D)

NORTH CAROLINA
- Burr, Richard (R)
- Tillis, Thom (R)

NORTH DAKOTA
- Heitkamp, Heidi (D)
- Hoeven, John (R)

OHIO
- Brown, Sherrod (D)
- Portman, Rob (R)

OKLAHOMA
- Inhofe, James M. (R)
- Lankford, James (R)

OREGON
- Merkley, Jeff (D)
- Wyden, Ron (D)

PENNSYLVANIA
- Casey, Robert P., Jr (D)
- Toomey, Pat (R)

RHODE ISLAND
- Reed, Jack (D)
- Whitehouse, Sheldon (D)

SOUTH CAROLINA
- Graham, Lindsey (R)
- Scott, Tim (R)

SOUTH DAKOTA
- Rounds, Mike (R)
- Thune, John (R)

TENNESSEE
- Alexander, Lamar (R)
- Corker, Bob (R)

TEXAS
- Cornyn, John (R)
- Cruz, Ted (R)

UTAH
- Lee, Mike (R)
- Hatch, Orrin G. (R)

VERMONT
- Leahy, Patrick J. (D)
- Sanders, Bernard (I)

VIRGINIA
- Kaine, Tim (D)
- Warner, Mark (D)

WASHINGTON
- Cantwell, Maria (D)
- Murray, Patty (D)

WEST VIRGINIA
- Capito, Shelley Moore (R)
- Manchin III, Joe (D)

WISCONSIN
- Baldwin, Tammy (D)
- Johnson, Ron (R)

WYOMING
- Barrasso, John (R)
- Enzi, Michael B. (R)

U.S. Representatives
(as of January 3, 2017)

. . . .

For information on how to contact your representative, please visit http://www.house.gov/representatives/find.

ALABAMA
- Aderholt, Robert (R)
- Brooks, Mo (R)
- Byrne, Bradley (R)
- Palmer, Gary (R)
- Roby, Martha (R)
- Rogers, Mike (R)
- Sewell, Terri (D)

ALASKA
- Young, Don (R) At-large

AMERICAN SAMOA
- Radewagen, Amata Coleman (R) (Delegate)

ARIZONA
- Biggs, Andy (R)
- Franks, Trent (R)
- Gallego, Ruben (D)
- Gosar, Paul (R)
- Grijalva, Raúl (D)
- McSally, Martha (R)
- O'Halleran, Tom (D)
- Schweikert, David (R)
- Sinema, Kyrsten (D)

ARKANSAS
- Crawford, Rick (R)
- Hill, French (R)
- Westerman, Bruce (R)
- Womack, Steve (R)

CALIFORNIA
- Aguilar, Pete (D)
- Barragán, Nanette (D)
- Bass, Karen (D)
- Becerra, Xavier (D)
- Bera, Ami (D)
- Brownley, Julia (D)
- Calvert, Ken (R)
- Carbajal, Salud (D)
- Cárdenas, Tony (D)

- Chu, Judy (D)
- Cook, Paul (R)
- Correa, Lou (D)
- Costa, Jim (D)
- Davis, Susan (D)
- Denham, Jeff (R)
- DeSaulnier, Mark (D)
- Eshoo, Anna (D)
- Garamendi, John (D)
- Huffman, Jared (D)
- Hunter, Duncan D. (R)
- Issa, Darrell (R)
- Khanna, Ro (D)
- Knight, Steve (R)
- LaMalfa, Doug (R)
- Lee, Barbara (D)
- Lieu, Ted (D)
- Lofgren, Zoe (D)
- Lowenthal, Alan (D)
- Matsui, Doris (D)
- McCarthy, Kevin (R)
- McClintock, Tom (R)
- McNerney, Jerry (D)
- Napolitano, Grace (D)
- Nunes, Devin (R)
- Panetta, Jimmy (D)
- Pelosi, Nancy (D)
- Peters, Scott (D)
- Rohrabacher, Dana (R)
- Roybal-Allard, Lucille (D)
- Royce, Ed (R)
- Ruiz, Raul (D)
- Sánchez, Linda (D)
- Schiff, Adam (D)

- Sherman, Brad (D)
- Speier, Jackie (D)
- Swalwell, Eric (D)
- Takano, Mark (D)
- Thompson, Mike (D)
- Torres, Norma (D)
- Valadao, David (R)
- Vargas, Juan (D)
- Walters, Mimi (R)
- Waters, Maxine (D)

COLORADO
- Buck, Ken (R)
- Coffman, Mike (R)
- DeGette, Diana (D)
- Lamborn, Doug (R)
- Perlmutter, Ed (D)
- Polis, Jared (D)
- Tipton, Scott (R)

CONNECTICUT
- Courtney, Joe (D)
- DeLauro, Rosa (D)
- Esty, Elizabeth (D)
- Himes, Jim (D)
- Larson, John B. (D)

DELAWARE
- Blunt Rochester, Lisa (D)
  At-large

DISTRICT OF COLUMBIA
- Norton, Eleanor Holmes (D) (Delegate)

FLORIDA
- Bilirakis, Gus (R)
- Buchanan, Vern (R)

- Castor, Kathy (D)
- Crist, Charlie (D)
- Curbelo, Carlos (R)
- Demings, Val (D)
- DeSantis, Ron (R)
- Deutch, Ted (D)
- Díaz-Balart, Mario (R)
- Dunn, Neal (R)
- Frankel, Lois (D)
- Gaetz, Matt (R)
- Hastings, Alcee (D)
- Lawson, Al (D)
- Mast, Brian (R)
- Murphy, Stephanie (D)
- Posey, Bill (R)
- Rooney, Francis (R)
- Rooney, Tom (R)
- Ros-Lehtinen, Ileana (R)
- Ross, Dennis A. (R)
- Rutherford, John (R)
- Soto, Darren (D)
- Wasserman
  Schultz, Debbie (D)
- Webster, Daniel (R)
- Wilson, Frederica (D)
- Yoho, Ted (R)

GEORGIA
- Allen, Rick W. (R)
- Bishop, Sanford (D)
- Carter, Buddy (R)
- Collins, Doug (R)
- Ferguson, Drew (R)
- Graves, Tom (R)
- Hice, Jody (R)
- Johnson, Hank (D)

- Lewis, John (D)
- Loudermilk, Barry (R)
- Price, Tom (R)
- Scott, Austin (R)
- Scott, David (D)
- Woodall, Rob (R)

GUAM
- Bordallo, Madeleine (D)

HAWAII
- Gabbard, Tulsi (D)
- Hanabusa, Colleen (D)

IDAHO
- Labrador, Raúl (R)
- Simpson, Mike (R)

ILLINOIS
- Bost, Mike (R)
- Bustos, Cheri (D)
- Davis, Danny K. (D)
- Davis, Rodney (R)
- Foster, Bill (D)
- Gutiérrez, Luis (D)
- Hultgren, Randy (R)
- Kelly, Robin (D)
- Kinzinger, Adam (R)
- Krishnamoorthi, Raja (D)
- LaHood, Darin (R)
- Lipinski, Dan (D)
- Quigley, Mike (D)
- Roskam, Peter (R)
- Rush, Bobby (D)
- Schakowsky, Jan (D)
- Schneider, Brad (D)
- Shimkus, John (R)

INDIANA
- Banks, Jim (R)
- Brooks, Susan (R)
- Bucshon, Larry (R)
- Carson, André (D)
- Hollingsworth, Trey (R)
- Messer, Luke (R)
- Rokita, Todd (R)
- Visclosky, Pete (D)
- Walorski, Jackie (R)

IOWA
- Blum, Rod (R)
- King, Steve (R)
- Loebsack, Dave (D)
- Young, David (R)

KANSAS
- Jenkins, Lynn (R)
- Marshall, Roger (R)
- Pompeo, Mike (R)
- Yoder, Kevin (R)

KENTUCKY
- Barr, Andy (R)
- Comer, James (R)
- Guthrie, Brett (R)
- Massie, Thomas (R)
- Rogers, Hal (R)
- Yarmuth, John (D)

LOUISIANA
- Abraham, Ralph (R)
- Graves, Garret (R)
- Higgins, Clay (R)
- Johnson, Mike (R)
- Richmond, Cedric (D)

- Scalise, Steve (R)

MAINE
- Pingree, Chellie (D)
- Poliquin, Bruce (R)

MARYLAND
- Brown, Anthony G. (D)
- Cummings, Elijah (D)
- Delaney, John (D)
- Harris, Andy (R)
- Hoyer, Steny (D)
- Raskin, Jamie (D)
- Ruppersberger, Dutch (D)
- Sarbanes, John (D)

MASSACHUSETTS
- Capuano, Mike (D)
- Clark, Katherine (D)
- Keating, Bill (D)
- Kennedy III, Joseph P. (D)
- Lynch, Stephen F. (D)
- McGovern, Jim (D)
- Moulton, Seth (D)
- Neal, Richard (D)
- Tsongas, Niki (D)

MICHIGAN
- Amash, Justin (R)
- Bergman, Jack (R)
- Bishop, Mike (R)
- Conyers, John (D)
- Dingell, Debbie (D)
- Huizenga, Bill (R)
- Kildee, Dan (D)
- Lawrence, Brenda (D)

- Levin, Sander (D)
- Mitchell, Paul (R)
- Moolenaar, John (R)
- Trott, Dave (R)
- Upton, Fred (R)
- Walberg, Tim (R)

MINNESOTA
- Ellison, Keith (D)
- Emmer, Tom (R)
- Lewis, Jason (R)
- McCollum, Betty (D)
- Nolan, Rick (D)
- Paulsen, Erik (R)
- Peterson, Collin (D)
- Walz, Tim (D)

MISSISSIPPI
- Harper, Gregg (R)
- Kelly, Trent (R)
- Palazzo, Steven (R)
- Thompson, Bennie (D)

MISSOURI
- Clay, Lacy (D)
- Cleaver, Emanuel (D)
- Graves, Sam (R)
- Hartzler, Vicky (R)
- Long, Billy (R)
- Luetkemeyer, Blaine (R)
- Smith, Jason T. (R)
- Wagner, Ann (R)

MONTANA
- Zinke, Ryan (R) At-large

NEBRASKA
- Bacon, Don (R)

- Fortenberry, Jeff (R)
- Smith, Adrian (R)

NEVADA
- Amodei, Mark (R)
- Kihuen, Ruben (D)
- Rosen, Jacky (D)
- Titus, Dina (D)

NEW HAMPSHIRE
- Kuster, Ann McLane (D)
- Shea-Porter, Carol (D)

NEW JERSEY
- Frelinghuysen, Rodney (R)
- Gottheimer, Josh (D)
- Lance, Leonard (R)
- LoBiondo, Frank (R)
- MacArthur, Tom (R)
- Norcross, Donald (D)
- Pallone, Frank (D)
- Pascrell, Bill (D)
- Payne, Donald, Jr. (D)
- Sires, Albio (D)
- Smith, Chris (R)
- Watson Coleman, Bonnie (D)

NEW MEXICO
- Luján, Ben Ray (D)
- Lujan Grisham, Michelle (D)
- Pearce, Steve (R)

NEW YORK
- Clarke, Yvette (D)
- Collins, Chris (R)

- Crowley, Joseph (D)
- Donovan, Dan (R)
- Engel, Eliot (D)
- Espaillat, Adriano (D)
- Faso, John (R)
- Higgins, Brian (D)
- Jeffries, Hakeem (D)
- Katko, John (R)
- King, Peter T. (R)
- Lowey, Nita (D)
- Maloney, Carolyn (D)
- Maloney, Sean Patrick (D)
- Meeks, Gregory (D)
- Meng, Grace (D)
- Nadler, Jerrold (D)
- Reed, Tom (R)
- Rice, Kathleen (D)
- Serrano, José E. (D)
- Slaughter, Louise (D)
- Stefanik, Elise (R)
- Suozzi, Thomas (D)
- Tenney, Claudia (R)
- Tonko, Paul (D)
- Velázquez, Nydia (D)
- Zeldin, Lee (R)

NORTH CAROLINA
- Adams, Alma (D)
- Budd, Ted (R)
- Butterfield, G. K. (D)
- Foxx, Virginia (R)
- Holding, George (R)
- Hudson, Richard (R)
- Jones, Walter B., Jr. (R)
- McHenry, Patrick (R)
- Meadows, Mark (R)

- Pittenger, Robert (R)
- Price, David (D)
- Rouzer, David (R)
- Walker, Mark (R)

NORTH DAKOTA
- Cramer, Kevin (R) At-large

NORTHERN MARIANA ISLANDS
- Sablan, Gregorio (I) (Delegate)

OHIO
- Beatty, Joyce (D)
- Chabot, Steve (R)
- Davidson, Warren (R)
- Fudge, Marcia (D)
- Gibbs, Bob (R)
- Johnson, Bill (R)
- Jordan, Jim (R)
- Joyce, David (R)
- Kaptur, Marcy (D)
- Latta, Bob (R)
- Renacci, Jim (R)
- Ryan, Tim (D)
- Stivers, Steve (R)
- Tiberi, Pat (R)
- Turner, Mike (R)
- Wenstrup, Brad (R)

OKLAHOMA
- Bridenstine, Jim (R)
- Cole, Tom (R)
- Lucas, Frank (R)
- Mullin, Markwayne (R)

- Russell, Steve (R)

- Blumenauer, Earl (D)
- Bonamici, Suzanne (D)
- DeFazio, Peter (D)
- Schrader, Kurt (D)
- Walden, Greg (R)

PENNSYLVANIA
- Barletta, Lou (R)
- Boyle, Brendan (D)
- Brady, Bob (D)
- Cartwright, Matt (D)
- Costello, Ryan (R)
- Dent, Charlie (R)
- Doyle, Michael F. (D)
- Evans, Dwight (D)
- Fitzpatrick, Brian (R)
- Kelly, Mike (R)
- Marino, Tom (R)
- Meehan, Pat (R)
- Murphy, Timothy F. (R)
- Perry, Scott (R)
- Rothfus, Keith (R)
- Shuster, Bill (R)
- Smucker, Lloyd (R)
- Thompson, Glenn (R)

PUERTO RICO
- González, Jenniffer (R) (Resident Commissioner)

RHODE ISLAND
- Cicilline, David (D)
- Langevin, James (D)

SOUTH CAROLINA
- Clyburn, Jim (D)
- Duncan, Jeff (R)
- Gowdy, Trey (R)
- Mulvaney, Mick (R)
- Rice, Tom (R)
- Sanford, Mark (R)
- Wilson, Joe (R)

SOUTH DAKOTA
- Noem, Kristi (R) At-large

TENNESSEE
- Black, Diane (R)
- Blackburn, Marsha (R)
- Cohen, Steve (D)
- Cooper, Jim (D)
- DesJarlais, Scott (R)
- Duncan, Jimmy (R)
- Fleischmann, Chuck (R)
- Kustoff, David (R)
- Roe, Phil (R)

TEXAS
- Arrington, Jodey (R)
- Babin, Brian (R)
- Barton, Joe (R)
- Brady, Kevin (R)
- Burgess, Michael C. (R)
- Carter, John (R)
- Castro, Joaquín (D)
- Conaway, Mike (R)
- Cuellar, Henry (D)
- Culberson, John (R)
- Doggett, Lloyd (D)
- Farenthold, Blake (R)
- Flores, Bill (R)

- Gohmert, Louie (R)
- González, Vicente (D)
- Granger, Kay (R)
- Green, Al (D)
- Green, Gene (D)
- Hensarling, Jeb (R)
- Hurd, Will (R)
- Jackson Lee, Sheila (D)
- Johnson, Eddie Bernice (D)
- Johnson, Sam (R)
- Marchant, Kenny (R)
- McCaul, Michael (R)
- O'Rourke, Beto (D)
- Olson, Pete (R)
- Poe, Ted (R)
- Ratcliffe, John (R)
- Sessions, Pete (R)
- Smith, Lamar S. (R)
- Thornberry, Mac (R)
- Veasey, Marc (D)
- Vela, Filemon, Jr. (D)
- Weber, Randy (R)
- Williams, Roger (R)

UTAH
- Bishop, Rob (R)
- Chaffetz, Jason (R)
- Love, Mia (R)
- Stewart, Chris (R)

VERMONT
- Welch, Peter (D) At-large

VIRGIN ISLANDS
- Plaskett, Stacey (D) (Delegate)

VIRGINIA
- Beyer, Don (D)
- Brat, Dave (R)
- Comstock, Barbara (R)
- Connolly, Gerry (D)
- Garrett, Thomas, Jr. (R)
- Goodlatte, Bob (R)
- Griffith, Morgan (R)
- McEachin, Donald (D)
- Scott, Bobby (D)
- Taylor, Scott (R)
- Wittman, Rob (R)

WASHINGTON
- DelBene, Suzan (D)
- Heck, Dennis (D)
- Herrera Beutler, Jaime (R)
- Jayapal, Pramila (D)
- Kilmer, Derek (D)
- Larsen, Rick (D)
- McMorris Rodgers, Cathy (R)
- Newhouse, Dan (R)
- Reichert, Dave (R)
- Smith, Adam (D)

WEST VIRGINIA
- Jenkins, Evan (R)
- McKinley, David (R)
- Mooney, Alex (R)

WISCONSIN
- Duffy, Sean (R)
- Gallagher, Mike (R)
- Grothman, Glenn (R)
- Kind, Ron (D)

- Moore, Gwen (D)
- Pocan, Mark (D)
- Ryan, Paul (R)
- Sensenbrenner, Jim (R)

WYOMING
- Cheney, Liz (R) At-large

APPENDIX D

U.S. Governors
(as of January 3, 2017)

. . . .

For information on how to contact your governor, please visit http://www.usa.gov/Contact/Governors.shtml.

ALABAMA
Robert J. Bentley (R)

ALASKA
Bill Walker (I)

ARIZONA
Doug Ducey (R)

ARKANSAS
Asa Hutchinson (R)

CALIFORNIA
Jerry Brown (D)

COLORADO
John Hickenlooper (D)

CONNECTICUT
Dannel Malloy (D)

DELAWARE
John Carney (D)

DISTRICT OF COLUMBIA
*Mayoralty
Muriel Bowder (D)

FLORIDA
Rick Scott (R)

GEORGIA
Nathan Deal (R)

HAWAII
David Ige (D)

IDAHO
Butch Otter (R)

ILLINOIS
~~Bruce Rauner (R)~~   PRITZER (D)

INDIANA
Eric Holcomb (R)

IOWA
Terry Branstad (R)

KANSAS
Sam Brownback (R)

KENTUCKY
Matt Bevin (R)

LOUISIANA
John Bel Edwards (D)

MAINE
Paul LePage (R)

MARYLAND
Larry Hogan (R)

MASSACHUSETTS
Charlie Baker (R)

MICHIGAN
Rick Snyder (R)

MINNESOTA
Mark Dayton (D)

MISSISSIPPI
Phil Bryant (R)

MISSOURI
Eric Greitens (R)

MONTANA
Steve Bullock (D)

NEBRASKA
Pete Ricketts (R)

NEVADA
Brian Sandoval (R)

NEW HAMPSHIRE
Chris Sununu (R)

NEW JERSEY
Chris Christie (R)

NEW MEXICO
Susana Martinez (R)

NEW YORK
Andrew Cuomo (D)

NORTH CAROLINA
Roy Cooper (D)

NORTH DAKOTA
Doug Burgum (R)

OHIO
~~John Kasich~~ (R)   Lewine

OKLAHOMA
Mary Fallin (R)

OREGON
Kate Brown (D)

PENNSYLVANIA
Tom Wolf (D)

RHODE ISLAND
Gina Raimondo (D)

SOUTH CAROLINA
Henry McMaster (R)

SOUTH DAKOTA
Dennis Daugaard (R)

TENNESSEE
Bill Haslam (R)

TEXAS
Greg Abbott (R)

UTAH
Gary Herbert (R)

VERMONT
Phil Scott (R)

VIRGINIA
Terry McAuliffe (D)

WASHINGTON
Jay Inslee (D)

WEST VIRGINIA
Jim Justice (D)

WISCONSIN
Scott Walker (R)

WYOMING
Matt Mead (R)

APPENDIX E

U.S. State Capitals

· ·

U.S. State, Possession, or Territory	Abbrev.	Capital
Alabama	AL	Montgomery
Alaska	AK	Juneau
American Samoa	AS	Pago Pago
Arizona	AZ	Phoenix
Arkansas	AR	Little Rock
California	CA	Sacramento
Colorado	CO	Denver
Connecticut	CT	Hartford
Delaware	DE	Dover
District of Columbia	DC	Washington
Federated States of Micronesia	FM	Palikir
Florida	FL	Tallahassee
Georgia	GA	Atlanta
Guam	GU	Hagatna (Agana)
Hawaii	HI	Honolulu
Idaho	ID	Boise
Illinois	IL	Springfield
Indiana	IN	Indianapolis
Iowa	IA	Des Moines
Kansas	KS	Topeka
Kentucky	KY	Frankfort

U.S. State, Possession, or Territory	Abbrev.	Capital
Louisiana	LA	Baton Rouge
Maine	ME	Augusta
Maryland	MD	Annapolis
Marshall Islands	MH	Majuro
Massachusetts	MA	Boston
Michigan	MI	Lansing
Minnesota	MN	St. Paul
Mississippi	MS	Jackson
Missouri	MO	Jefferson City
Montana	MT	Helena
Nebraska	NE	Lincoln
Nevada	NV	Carson City
New Hampshire	NH	Concord
New Jersey	NJ	Trenton
New Mexico	NM	Santa Fe
New York	NY	Albany
North Carolina	NC	Raleigh
North Dakota	ND	Bismarck
Northern Mariana Islands	MP	Saipan
Ohio	OH	Columbus
Oklahoma	OK	Oklahoma City
Oregon	OR	Salem
Palau	PW	Koror
Pennsylvania	PA	Harrisburg
Puerto Rico	PR	San Juan
Rhode Island	RI	Providence
South Carolina	SC	Columbia
South Dakota	SD	Pierre
Tennessee	TN	Nashville
Texas	TX	Austin
Utah	UT	Salt Lake City
Vermont	VT	Montpelier

U.S. State, Possession, or Territory	Abbrev.	Capital
Virginia	VA	Richmond
Virgin Islands	VI	St. Thomas
Washington	WA	Olympia
West Virginia	WV	Charleston
Wisconsin	WI	Madison
Wyoming	WY	Cheyenne

APPENDIX F

The Declaration of Independence

∙∙

IN CONGRESS, July 4, 1776.

The unanimous Declaration of the thirteen united States of America,

When in the Course of human events, it becomes necessary for one people to dissolve the political bands which have connected them with another, and to assume among the powers of the earth, the separate and equal station to which the Laws of Nature and of Nature's God entitle them, a decent respect to the opinions of mankind requires that they should declare the causes which impel them to the separation.

We hold these truths to be self-evident, that all men are created equal, that they are endowed by their Creator with certain unalienable Rights, that among these are Life, Liberty and the pursuit of Happiness.—That to secure these rights, Governments are instituted among Men, deriving their just powers from the consent of the governed,—That whenever any Form of Government becomes destructive of these ends, it is the Right of the People to alter or to abolish it, and to institute a new Government, laying its foundation on such principles and organizing its powers in such form, as to them shall seem most likely to effect their Safety and Happiness. Prudence, indeed, will dictate that Governments long established should not be changed for light and transient causes; and accordingly all experience hath shewn, that mankind are more disposed to suffer, while evils are sufferable, than to right themselves by abolishing the forms to which they are accustomed. But when a long train of abuses and usurpations, pursuing invariably the same Object evinces a design to reduce them under absolute Despotism, it is their right, it is their duty, to throw off such Government, and to provide new Guards for their future security.—Such has been the patient sufferance of these Colonies; and such is now the necessity which constrains them to alter their former Systems of Government. The history of the present King of Great Britain is a history of repeated injuries and usurpations, all having in direct object the establishment of an absolute Tyranny over these States. To prove this, let Facts be submitted to a candid world.

He has refused his Assent to Laws, the most wholesome and necessary for the public good.

He has forbidden his Governors to pass Laws of immediate and pressing importance, unless suspended in their operation till his Assent should be obtained; and when so suspended, he has utterly neglected to attend to them.

He has refused to pass other Laws for the accommodation of large districts of people, unless those people would relinquish the right of Representation in the Legislature, a right inestimable to them and formidable to tyrants only.

He has called together legislative bodies at places unusual, uncomfortable, and distant from the depository of their public Records, for the sole purpose of fatiguing them into compliance with his measures.

He has dissolved Representative Houses repeatedly, for opposing with manly firmness his invasions on the rights of the people.

He has refused for a long time, after such dissolutions, to cause others to be elected; whereby the Legislative powers, incapable of Annihilation, have returned to the People at large for their exercise; the State remaining in the mean time exposed to all the dangers of invasion from without, and convulsions within.

He has endeavoured to prevent the population of these States; for that purpose obstructing the Laws for Naturalization of Foreigners; refusing to pass others to encourage their migrations hither, and raising the conditions of new Appropriations of Lands.

He has obstructed the Administration of Justice, by refusing his Assent to Laws for establishing Judiciary powers.

He has made Judges dependent on his Will alone, for the tenure of their offices, and the amount and payment of their salaries.

He has erected a multitude of New Offices, and sent hither swarms of Officers to harrass our people, and eat out their substance.

He has kept among us, in times of peace, Standing Armies without the Consent of our legislatures.

He has affected to render the Military independent of and superior to the Civil power.

He has combined with others to subject us to a jurisdiction foreign to our constitution, and unacknowledged by our laws; giving his Assent to their Acts of pretended Legislation:

For Quartering large bodies of armed troops among us;

For protecting them, by a mock Trial, from punishment for any Murders which they should commit on the Inhabitants of these States;

For cutting off our Trade with all parts of the world;

For imposing Taxes on us without our Consent;

For depriving us in many cases, of the benefits of Trial by Jury;

For transporting us beyond Seas to be tried for pretended offences;

For abolishing the free System of English Laws in a neighbouring Province, establishing therein an Arbitrary government, and enlarging its Boundaries so as to render it at once an example and fit instrument for introducing the same absolute rule into these Colonies;

For taking away our Charters, abolishing our most valuable Laws, and altering fundamentally the Forms of our Governments;

For suspending our own Legislatures, and declaring themselves invested with power to legislate for us in all cases whatsoever.

He has abdicated Government here, by declaring us out of his Protection and waging War against us.

He has plundered our seas, ravaged our Coasts, burnt our towns, and destroyed the lives of our people.

He is at this time transporting large Armies of foreign Mercenaries to compleat the works of death, desolation and tyranny, already begun with circumstances of Cruelty & perfidy scarcely paralleled in the most barbarous ages, and totally unworthy the Head of a civilized nation.

He has constrained our fellow Citizens taken Captive on the high Seas to bear Arms against their Country, to become the executioners of their friends and Brethren, or to fall themselves by their Hands.

He has excited domestic insurrections amongst us, and has endeavoured to bring on the inhabitants of our frontiers, the merciless Indian Savages, whose known rule of warfare, is an undistinguished destruction of all ages, sexes and conditions.

In every stage of these Oppressions We have Petitioned for Redress in the most humble terms: Our repeated Petitions have been answered only by repeated injury. A Prince whose character is thus marked by every act which may define a Tyrant, is unfit to be the ruler of a free people.

Nor have We been wanting in attentions to our British brethren. We have warned them from time to time of attempts by their legislature to extend an unwarrantable jurisdiction over us. We have reminded them of the circumstances of our emigration and settlement here. We have appealed to their native justice and magnanimity, and we have conjured them by the ties of our common kindred to disavow these usurpations, which would inevitably interrupt our connections and correspondence. They too have been deaf to the voice of justice and of consanguinity. We must, therefore, acquiesce in the necessity, which denounces our Separation, and hold them, as we hold the rest of mankind, Enemies in War, in Peace Friends.

We, therefore, the Representatives of the united States of America, in General Congress, Assembled, appealing to the Supreme Judge of the world for the rectitude of our intentions, do, in the Name, and by Authority of the good People of these Colonies, solemnly publish and declare, That these United Colonies are, and of Right ought to be Free and Independent States; that they are Absolved from all Allegiance to the British Crown, and that all political connection between them and the State of Great Britain, is and ought to be totally dissolved; and that as Free and Independent States, they have full Power to levy War, conclude Peace, contract Alliances, establish Commerce, and to do all other Acts and Things which Independent States may of right do. And for the support of this Declaration, with a firm reliance on the protection of divine Providence, we mutually pledge to each other our Lives, our Fortunes and our sacred Honor.

The 56 signatures on the Declaration appear in the positions indicated:

Column 1

GEORGIA
Button Gwinnett
Lyman Hall
George Walton

Column 2

NORTH CAROLINA
William Hooper
Joseph Hewes
John Penn

SOUTH CAROLINA
Edward Rutledge
Thomas Heyward, Jr.
Thomas Lynch, Jr.
Arthur Middleton

Column 3

MASSACHUSETTS
John Hancock

MARYLAND
Samuel Chase
William Paca
Thomas Stone
Charles Carroll of
   Carrollton

VIRGINIA
George Wythe
Richard Henry Lee
Thomas Jefferson
Benjamin Harrison

Thomas Nelson, Jr.
Francis Lightfoot Lee
Carter Braxton

Column 4

PENNSYLVANIA
Robert Morris
Benjamin Rush
Benjamin Franklin
John Morton
George Clymer
James Smith
George Taylor
James Wilson
George Ross

DELAWARE
Caesar Rodney
George Read
Thomas McKean

Column 5

NEW YORK
William Floyd
Philip Livingston
Francis Lewis
Lewis Morris

NEW JERSEY
Richard Stockton
John Witherspoon
Francis Hopkinson
John Hart
Abraham Clark

Column 6

NEW HAMPSHIRE
Josiah Bartlett
William Whipple

MASSACHUSETTS
Samuel Adams
John Adams
Robert Treat Paine
Elbridge Gerry

RHODE ISLAND
Stephen Hopkins
William Ellery

CONNECTICUT
Roger Sherman
Samuel Huntington
William Williams
Oliver Wolcott

NEW HAMPSHIRE
Matthew Thornton

APPENDIX G

The U.S. Constitution

. . . .

NOTE: *Italicized sections or clauses were later superseded by amendments.*

WE THE PEOPLE of the United States, in Order to form a more perfect Union, establish Justice, insure domestic Tranquility, provide for the common defense, promote the general Welfare, and secure the Blessings of Liberty to ourselves and our Posterity, do ordain and establish this Constitution for the United States of America.

ARTICLE I

Section 1

All legislative Powers herein granted shall be vested in a Congress of the United States, which shall consist of a Senate and House of Representatives.

Section 2

1. The House of Representatives shall be composed of Members chosen every second Year by the People of the several States, and the Electors in each State shall have the Qualifications requisite for Electors of the most numerous Branch of the State Legislature.

2. No Person shall be a Representative who shall not have attained to the Age of twenty five Years, and been seven Years a Citizen of the United States, and who shall not, when elected, be an Inhabitant of that State in which he shall be chosen.

3. *Representatives and direct Taxes shall be apportioned among the several States which may be included within this Union, according to their respective Numbers, which shall be determined by adding to the whole Number of free Persons, including those bound to Service for a Term of Years, and excluding Indians not taxed, three fifths of all other Persons.* The actual Enumeration shall be made within three Years after the first Meeting of the Congress of the United States, and within every subsequent Term of ten Years, in such Manner as they shall by Law direct. The Number of Representatives shall not exceed one for every thirty Thousand, but each State shall have at Least one Representative; and until such enumeration shall be made, the State of New Hampshire shall be entitled to choose three, Massachusetts eight, Rhode Island and Providence Plantations one, Connecticut five, New York six, New Jersey four, Pennsylvania eight, Delaware one, Maryland six, Virginia ten, North Carolina five, South Carolina five, and Georgia three.

4. When vacancies happen in the Representation from any State, the Executive Authority thereof shall issue Writs of Election to fill such Vacancies.

5. The House of Representatives shall choose their Speaker and other Officers; and shall have the sole Power of Impeachment.

Section 3

1. The Senate of the United States shall be composed of two Senators from each State, *chosen by the Legislature* thereof for six Years; and each Senator shall have one Vote.

2. Immediately after they shall be assembled in Consequence of the first Election, they shall be divided as equally as may be into three Classes. The Seats of the Senators of the

first Class shall be vacated at the Expiration of the second Year, of the second Class at the Expiration of the fourth Year, and of the third Class at the Expiration of the sixth Year, so that one third may be chosen every second Year; *and if Vacancies happen by Resignation, or otherwise, during the Recess of the Legislature of any State, the Executive thereof may make temporary Appointments until the next Meeting of the Legislature, which shall then fill such Vacancies.*

3. No Person shall be a Senator who shall not have attained to the Age of thirty Years, and been nine Years a Citizen of the United States, and who shall not, when elected, be an Inhabitant of that State for which he shall be chosen.

4. The Vice President of the United States shall be President of the Senate, but shall have no Vote, unless they be equally divided.

5. The Senate shall choose their other Officers, and also a President pro tempore, in the Absence of the Vice President, or when he shall exercise the Office of President of the United States.

6. The Senate shall have the sole Power to try all Impeachments. When sitting for that Purpose, they shall be on Oath or Affirmation. When the President of the United States is tried, the Chief Justice shall preside: And no Person shall be convicted without the Concurrence of two thirds of the Members present.

7. Judgment in Cases of Impeachment shall not extend further than to removal from Office, and disqualification to hold and enjoy any Office of honor, Trust or Profit under the United States: but the Party convicted shall nevertheless be liable and subject to Indictment, Trial, Judgment and Punishment, according to Law.

Section 4

1. The Times, Places and Manner of holding Elections for Senators and Representatives shall be prescribed in each State by the Legislature thereof; but the Congress may at any

time by Law make or alter such Regulations, except as to the Places of choosing Senators.

2. The Congress shall assemble at least once in every Year, and such Meeting shall *be on the first Monday in December*, unless they shall by Law appoint a different Day.

Section 5

1. Each House shall be the Judge of the Elections, Returns and Qualifications of its own Members, and a Majority of each shall constitute a Quorum to do Business; but a smaller Number may adjourn from day to day, and may be authorized to compel the Attendance of absent Members, in such Manner, and under such Penalties as each House may provide.

2. Each House may determine the Rules of its Proceedings, punish its Members for disorderly Behaviour, and, with the Concurrence of two thirds, expel a Member.

3. Each House shall keep a Journal of its Proceedings, and from time to time publish the same, excepting such Parts as may in their Judgment require Secrecy; and the Yeas and Nays of the Members of either House on any question shall, at the Desire of one fifth of those Present, be entered on the Journal.

4. Neither House, during the Session of Congress, shall, without the Consent of the other, adjourn for more than three days, nor to any other Place than that in which the two Houses shall be sitting.

Section 6

1. The Senators and Representatives shall receive a Compensation for their Services, to be ascertained by Law, and paid out of the Treasury of the United States. They shall in all Cases, except Treason, Felony and Breach of the Peace, be privileged from Arrest during their Attendance at the Session of their respective Houses, and in going to and returning from the same; and for any Speech or Debate in either House, they shall not be questioned in any other Place.

2. No Senator or Representative shall, during the Time for which he was elected, be appointed to any civil Office under the Authority of the United States, which shall have been created, or the Emoluments whereof shall have been increased during such time; and no Person holding any Office under the United States, shall be a Member of either House during his Continuance in Office.

Section 7

1. All Bills for raising Revenue shall originate in the House of Representatives; but the Senate may propose or concur with Amendments as on other Bills.

2. Every Bill which shall have passed the House of Representatives and the Senate, shall, before it become a Law, be presented to the President of the United States: If he approve he shall sign it, but if not he shall return it, with his Objections to that House in which it shall have originated, who shall enter the Objections at large on their Journal, and proceed to reconsider it. If after such Reconsideration two thirds of that House shall agree to pass the Bill, it shall be sent, together with the Objections, to the other House, by which it shall likewise be reconsidered, and if approved by two thirds of that House, it shall become a Law. But in all such Cases the Votes of both Houses shall be determined by yeas and Nays, and the Names of the Persons voting for and against the Bill shall be entered on the Journal of each House respectively. If any Bill shall not be returned by the President within ten Days (Sundays excepted) after it shall have been presented to him, the Same shall be a Law, in like Manner as if he had signed it, unless the Congress by their Adjournment prevent its Return, in which Case it shall not be a Law.

3. Every Order, Resolution, or Vote to which the Concurrence of the Senate and House of Representatives may be necessary (except on a question of Adjournment) shall be presented to the President of the United States; and before

the Same shall take Effect, shall be approved by him, or being disapproved by him, shall be repassed by two thirds of the Senate and House of Representatives, according to the Rules and Limitations prescribed in the Case of a Bill.

Section 8

The Congress shall have Power

1. To lay and collect Taxes, Duties, Imposts and Excises, to pay the Debts and provide for the common Defence and general Welfare of the United States; but all Duties, Imposts and Excises shall be uniform throughout the United States;

2. To borrow Money on the credit of the United States;

3. To regulate Commerce with foreign Nations, and among the several States, and with the Indian Tribes;

4. To establish a uniform Rule of Naturalization, and uniform Laws on the subject of Bankruptcies throughout the United States;

5. To coin Money, regulate the Value thereof, and of foreign Coin, and fix the Standard of Weights and Measures;

6. To provide for the Punishment of counterfeiting the Securities and current Coin of the United States;

7. To establish Post Offices and post Roads;

8. To promote the Progress of Science and useful Arts, by securing for limited Times to Authors and Inventors the exclusive Right to their respective Writings and Discoveries;

9. To constitute Tribunals inferior to the supreme Court;

10. To define and punish Piracies and Felonies committed on the high Seas, and Offences against the Law of Nations;

11. To declare War, grant Letters of Marque and Reprisal, and make Rules concerning Captures on Land and Water;

12. To raise and support Armies, but no Appropriation of Money to that Use shall be for a longer Term than two Years;

13. To provide and maintain a Navy;

14. To make Rules for the Government and Regulation of the land and naval Forces;

15. To provide for calling forth the Militia to execute the Laws of the Union, suppress Insurrections and repel Invasions;

16. To provide for organizing, arming, and disciplining, the Militia, and for governing such Part of them as may be employed in the Service of the United States, reserving to the States respectively, the Appointment of the Officers, and the Authority of training the Militia according to the discipline prescribed by Congress;

17. To exercise exclusive Legislation in all Cases whatsoever, over such District (not exceeding ten Miles square) as may, by Cession of particular States, and the Acceptance of Congress, become the Seat of the Government of the United States, and to exercise like Authority over all Places purchased by the Consent of the Legislature of the State in which the Same shall be, for the Erection of Forts, Magazines, Arsenals, dock-Yards, and other needful Buildings;—And

18. To make all Laws which shall be necessary and proper for carrying into Execution the foregoing Powers, and all other Powers vested by this Constitution in the Government of the United States, or in any Department or Officer thereof.

Section 9

1. The Migration or Importation of such Persons as any of the States now existing shall think proper to admit, shall not be prohibited by the Congress prior to the Year one thousand eight hundred and eight, but a Tax or duty may be imposed on such Importation, not exceeding ten dollars for each Person.

2. The Privilege of the Writ of Habeas Corpus shall not be suspended, unless when in Cases of Rebellion or Invasion the public Safety may require it.

3. No Bill of Attainder or ex post facto Law shall be passed.

4. No Capitation, or other direct, Tax shall be laid, *unless in Proportion to the Census or enumeration herein before directed to be taken.*

5. No Tax or Duty shall be laid on Articles exported from any State.

6. No Preference shall be given by any Regulation of Commerce or Revenue to the Ports of one State over those of another; nor shall Vessels bound to, or from, one State, be obliged to enter, clear, or pay Duties in another.

7. No Money shall be drawn from the Treasury, but in Consequence of Appropriations made by Law; and a regular Statement and Account of the Receipts and Expenditures of all public Money shall be published from time to time.

8. No Title of Nobility shall be granted by the United States: And no Person holding any Office of Profit or Trust under them, shall, without the Consent of the Congress, accept of any present, Emolument, Office, or Title, of any kind whatever, from any King, Prince, or foreign State.

Section 10

1. No State shall enter into any Treaty, Alliance, or Confederation; grant Letters of Marque and Reprisal; coin Money; emit Bills of Credit; make any Thing but gold and silver Coin a Tender in Payment of Debts; pass any Bill of Attainder, ex post facto Law, or Law impairing the Obligation of Contracts, or grant any Title of Nobility.

2. No State shall, without the Consent of the Congress, lay any Imposts or Duties on Imports or Exports, except what may be absolutely necessary for executing its inspection Laws: and the net Produce of all Duties and Imposts, laid by any State on Imports or Exports, shall be for the Use of the Treasury of the United States; and all such Laws shall be subject to the Revision and Controul of the Congress.

3. No State shall, without the Consent of Congress, lay any Duty of Tonnage, keep Troops, or Ships of War in time of Peace, enter into any Agreement or Compact with another State, or with a foreign Power, or engage in War, unless actually invaded, or in such imminent Danger as will not admit of delay.

ARTICLE II

Section 1

1. The executive Power shall be vested in a President of the United States of America. He shall hold his Office during the Term of four Years, and, together with the Vice President, chosen for the same Term, be elected, as follows:

2. Each State shall appoint, in such Manner as the Legislature thereof may direct, a Number of Electors, equal to the whole Number of Senators and Representatives to which the State may be entitled in the Congress: but no Senator or Representative, or Person holding an Office of Trust or Profit under the United States, shall be appointed an Elector.

3. *The Electors shall meet in their respective States, and vote by Ballot for two Persons, of whom one at least shall not be an Inhabitant of the same State with themselves. And they shall make a List of all the Persons voted for, and of the Number of Votes for each; which List they shall sign and certify, and transmit sealed to the Seat of the Government of the United States, directed to the President of the Senate. The President of the Senate shall, in the Presence of the Senate and House of Representatives, open all the Certificates, and the Votes shall then be counted. The Person having the greatest Number of Votes shall be the President, if such Number be a Majority of the whole Number of Electors appointed; and if there be more than one who have such Majority, and have an equal Number of Votes, then the House of Representatives shall immediately choose by Ballot one of them for President; and if no Person have a Majority, then from the five highest on the List the said House shall in like Manner choose the President. But in choosing the President, the Votes shall be taken by States, the Representation from each State having one Vote; A quorum for this purpose shall consist of a Member or Members from two thirds of the States, and a Majority of all the States shall be necessary to a Choice. In every Case, after the Choice of the President, the Person having the greatest Number of Votes of the Electors shall be the Vice President. But if there*

should remain two or more who have equal Votes, the Senate shall choose from them by Ballot the Vice President.

4. The Congress may determine the Time of choosing the Electors, and the Day on which they shall give their Votes; which Day shall be the same throughout the United States.

5. No Person except a natural born Citizen, or a Citizen of the United States, at the time of the Adoption of this Constitution, shall be eligible to the Office of President; neither shall any Person be eligible to that Office who shall not have attained to the Age of thirty five Years, and been fourteen Years a Resident within the United States.

6. *In Case of the Removal of the President from Office, or of his Death, Resignation, or Inability to discharge the Powers and Duties of the said Office, the Same shall devolve on the Vice President, and the Congress may by Law provide for the Case of Removal, Death, Resignation, or Inability, both of the President and Vice President, declaring what Officer shall then act as President, and such Officer shall act accordingly, until the Disability be removed, or a President shall be elected.*

7. The President shall, at stated Times, receive for his Services, a Compensation, which shall neither be increased nor diminished during the Period for which he shall have been elected, and he shall not receive within that Period any other Emolument from the United States, or any of them.

8. Before he enter on the Execution of his Office, he shall take the following Oath or Affirmation: —"I do solemnly swear (or affirm) that I will faithfully execute the Office of President of the United States, and will to the best of my Ability, preserve, protect and defend the Constitution of the United States."

Section 2

1. The President shall be Commander in Chief of the Army and Navy of the United States, and of the Militia of

the several States, when called into the actual Service of the United States; he may require the Opinion, in writing, of the principal Officer in each of the executive Departments, upon any Subject relating to the Duties of their respective Offices, and he shall have Power to grant Reprieves and Pardons for Offences against the United States, except in Cases of Impeachment.

2. He shall have Power, by and with the Advice and Consent of the Senate, to make Treaties, provided two thirds of the Senators present concur; and he shall nominate, and by and with the Advice and Consent of the Senate, shall appoint Ambassadors, other public Ministers and Consuls, Judges of the supreme Court, and all other Officers of the United States, whose Appointments are not herein otherwise provided for, and which shall be established by Law: but the Congress may by Law vest the Appointment of such inferior Officers, as they think proper, in the President alone, in the Courts of Law, or in the Heads of Departments.

3. The President shall have Power to fill up all Vacancies that may happen during the Recess of the Senate, by granting Commissions which shall expire at the End of their next Session.

Section 3

He shall from time to time give to the Congress Information of the State of the Union, and recommend to their Consideration such Measures as he shall judge necessary and expedient; he may, on extraordinary Occasions, convene both Houses, or either of them, and in Case of Disagreement between them, with Respect to the Time of Adjournment, he may adjourn them to such Time as he shall think proper; he shall receive Ambassadors and other public Ministers; he shall take Care that the Laws be faithfully executed, and shall Commission all the Officers of the United States.

Section 4

The President, Vice President and all civil Officers of the United States, shall be removed from Office on Impeachment for, and Conviction of, Treason, Bribery, or other high Crimes and Misdemeanors.

ARTICLE III

Section 1

The judicial Power of the United States shall be vested in one supreme Court, and in such inferior Courts as the Congress may from time to time ordain and establish. The Judges, both of the supreme and inferior Courts, shall hold their Offices during good Behaviour, and shall, at stated Times, receive for their Services a Compensation, which shall not be diminished during their Continuance in Office.

Section 2

1. The judicial Power shall extend to all Cases, in Law and Equity, arising under this Constitution, the Laws of the United States, and Treaties made, or which shall be made, under their Authority;—to all Cases affecting Ambassadors, other public Ministers and Consuls;—to all Cases of admiralty and maritime Jurisdiction;—to Controversies to which the United States shall be a Party;—to Controversies between two or more States;—*between a State and Citizens of another State*;—between Citizens of different States;—between Citizens of the same State claiming Lands under Grants of different States, and between a State, or the Citizens thereof, and foreign States, Citizens or Subjects.

2. In all Cases affecting Ambassadors, other public Ministers and Consuls, and those in which a State shall be Party, the supreme Court shall have original Jurisdiction. In all the other Cases before mentioned, the supreme Court shall have appellate Jurisdiction, both as to Law and Fact, with such

Exceptions, and under such Regulations as the Congress shall make.

3. The Trial of all Crimes, except in Cases of Impeachment, shall be by Jury; and such Trial shall be held in the State where the said Crimes shall have been committed; but when not committed within any State, the Trial shall be at such Place or Places as the Congress may by Law have directed.

Section 3

1. Treason against the United States, shall consist only in levying War against them, or in adhering to their Enemies, giving them Aid and Comfort. No Person shall be convicted of Treason unless on the Testimony of two Witnesses to the same overt Act, or on Confession in open Court.

2. The Congress shall have Power to declare the Punishment of Treason, but no Attainder of Treason shall work Corruption of Blood, or Forfeiture except during the Life of the Person attained.

ARTICLE IV

Section 1

Full Faith and Credit shall be given in each State to the public Acts, Records, and judicial Proceedings of every other State. And the Congress may by general Laws prescribe the Manner in which such Acts, Records and Proceedings shall be proved, and the Effect thereof.

Section 2

1. The Citizens of each State shall be entitled to all Privileges and Immunities of Citizens in the several States.

2. A Person charged in any State with Treason, Felony, or other Crime, who shall flee from Justice, and be found in another State, shall on Demand of the executive Authority of the State from which he fled, be delivered up, to be removed to the State having Jurisdiction of the Crime.

3. *No Person held to Service or Labour in one State, under the Laws thereof, escaping into another, shall, in Consequence of any Law or Regulation therein, be discharged from such Service or Labour, but shall be delivered up on Claim of the Party to whom such Service or Labour may be due.*

Section 3

1. New States may be admitted by the Congress into this Union; but no new State shall be formed or erected within the Jurisdiction of any other State; nor any State be formed by the Junction of two or more States, or Parts of States, without the Consent of the Legislatures of the States concerned as well as of the Congress.

2. The Congress shall have Power to dispose of and make all needful Rules and Regulations respecting the Territory or other Property belonging to the United States; and nothing in this Constitution shall be so construed as to Prejudice any Claims of the United States, or of any particular State.

Section 4

The United States shall guarantee to every State in this Union a Republican Form of Government, and shall protect each of them against Invasion; and on Application of the Legislature, or of the Executive (when the Legislature cannot be convened), against domestic Violence.

ARTICLE V

The Congress, whenever two thirds of both Houses shall deem it necessary, shall propose Amendments to this Constitution, or, on the Application of the Legislatures of two thirds of the several States, shall call a Convention for proposing Amendments, which, in either Case, shall be valid to all Intents and Purposes, as Part of this Constitution, when ratified by the Legislatures of three fourths of the several States, or by Conventions in three fourths thereof, as the one or the other Mode of Ratification may be proposed by the Congress; Provided that no Amendment which may be made prior to the Year One thousand eight hundred and eight shall in any Manner affect the first and fourth Clauses in the Ninth Section of the first Article; and that no State, without its Consent, shall be deprived of its equal Suffrage in the Senate.

ARTICLE VI

1. All Debts contracted and Engagements entered into, before the Adoption of this Constitution, shall be as valid against the United States under this Constitution, as under the Confederation.

2. This Constitution, and the Laws of the United States which shall be made in Pursuance thereof; and all Treaties made, or which shall be made, under the Authority of the United States, shall be the supreme Law of the Land; and the Judges in every State shall be bound thereby, any Thing in the Constitution or Laws of any State to the Contrary notwithstanding.

3. The Senators and Representatives before mentioned, and the Members of the several State Legislatures, and all executive and judicial Officers, both of the United States and of the several States, shall be bound by Oath or Affirmation, to support this Constitution; but no religious Test shall ever be required as a Qualification to any Office or public Trust under the United States.

ARTICLE VII

The Ratification of the Conventions of nine States, shall be sufficient for the Establishment of this Constitution between the States so ratifying the Same.

Done in Convention by the Unanimous Consent of the States present the Seventeenth Day of September in the Year of our Lord one thousand seven hundred and Eighty seven and of the Independence of the United States of America the

Twelfth. In witness whereof We have hereunto subscribed our Names,

G°. Washington
Presidt. and deputy from Virginia

DELAWARE
Geo: Read
Gunning Bedford jun.
John Dickinson
Richard Bassett
Jaco: Broom

MARYLAND
James McHenry
Dan of St Thos. Jenifer
Danl. Carroll

VIRGINIA
John Blair
James Madison Jr.

NORTH CAROLINA
Wm. Blount
Richd. Dobbs Spaight
Hu Williamson

SOUTH CAROLINA
J. Rutledge
Charles Cotesworth Pinckney
Charles Pinckney
Pierce Butler

GEORGIA
William Few
Abr Baldwin

NEW HAMPSHIRE
John Langdon
Nicholas Gilman

MASSACHUSETTS
Nathaniel Gorham
Rufus King

CONNECTICUT
Wm. Saml. Johnson
Roger Sherman

NEW YORK
Alexander Hamilton

NEW JERSEY
Wil: Livingston
David Brearley
Wm. Paterson
Jona: Dayton

PENNSYLVANIA
B. Franklin
Thomas Mifflin
Robt. Morris
Geo. Clymer
Thos. FitzSimons
Jared Ingersoll
James Wilson
Gouv Morris

The Bill of Rights

• •

NOTE: *The following text is a transcription of the first ten Amendments to the Constitution in their original form. These Amendments were ratified December 15, 1791, and form what is known as the "Bill of Rights."*

AMENDMENT I

Congress shall make no law respecting an establishment of religion, or prohibiting the free exercise thereof; or abridging the freedom of speech, or of the press; or the right of the people peaceably to assemble, and to petition the Government for a redress of grievances.

AMENDMENT II

A well regulated Militia, being necessary to the security of a free State, the right of the people to keep and bear Arms, shall not be infringed.

AMENDMENT III

No Soldier shall, in time of peace be quartered in any house, without the consent of the Owner, nor in time of war, but in a manner to be prescribed by law.

AMENDMENT IV

The right of the people to be secure in their persons, houses, papers, and effects, against unreasonable searches and seizures, shall not be violated, and no Warrants shall issue, but upon probable cause, supported by Oath or affirmation, and particularly describing the place to be searched, and the persons or things to be seized.

AMENDMENT V

No person shall be held to answer for a capital, or otherwise infamous crime, unless on a presentment or indictment of a Grand Jury, except in cases arising in the land or naval forces, or in the Militia, when in actual service in time of War or public danger; nor shall any person be subject for the same offence to be twice put in jeopardy of life or limb; nor shall be compelled in any criminal case to be a witness against himself, nor be deprived of life, liberty, or property, without due process of law; nor shall private property be taken for public use, without just compensation.

AMENDMENT VI

In all criminal prosecutions, the accused shall enjoy the right to a speedy and public trial, by an impartial jury of the State and district wherein the crime shall have been committed, which district shall have been previously ascertained by law, and to be informed of the nature and cause of the accusation; to be confronted with the witnesses against him; to have compulsory process for obtaining witnesses in his favor, and to have the Assistance of Counsel for his defence.

AMENDMENT VII

In Suits at common law, where the value in controversy shall exceed twenty dollars, the right of trial by jury shall be preserved, and no fact tried by a jury, shall be otherwise re-examined in any Court of the United States, than according to the rules of the common law.

AMENDMENT VIII

Excessive bail shall not be required, nor excessive fines imposed, nor cruel and unusual punishments inflicted.

Amendment IX

The enumeration in the Constitution, of certain rights, shall not be construed to deny or disparage others retained by the people.

Amendment X

The powers not delegated to the United States by the Constitution, nor prohibited by it to the States, are reserved to the States respectively, or to the people.

Amendments XI–XXVII

. . . .

Constitutional Amendments I–X make up what is known as the Bill of Rights. *Amendments XI–XXVII are listed below.*

AMENDMENT XI

Passed by Congress March 4, 1794. Ratified February 7, 1795.

NOTE: *Article III, Section 2, of the Constitution was modified by the Eleventh Amendment.*

The Judicial power of the United States shall not be construed to extend to any suit in law or equity, commenced or prosecuted against one of the United States by Citizens of another State, or by Citizens or Subjects of any Foreign State.

AMENDMENT XII

Passed by Congress December 9, 1803. Ratified June 15, 1804.

NOTE: *A portion of Article II, Section 1 of the Constitution was superseded by the Twelfth Amendment.*

The Electors shall meet in their respective states and vote by ballot for President and Vice-President, one of whom, at least, shall not be an inhabitant of the same state with themselves; they shall name in their ballots the person voted for as President, and in distinct ballots the person voted for as Vice-President, and they shall make distinct lists of all persons voted for as President, and of all persons voted for as Vice-President, and of the number of votes for each, which lists they shall sign and certify, and transmit sealed to the seat of the government of the United States, directed to the President of the Senate;——the President of the Senate shall, in the presence of the Senate and House of Representatives, open all the certificates and the votes shall then be counted;——The person having the greatest number of votes for President, shall be the President, if such number be a majority of the whole number of Electors appointed; and if no person have such majority, then from the persons having the highest numbers not exceeding three on the list of those voted for as President, the House of Representatives shall choose immediately, by ballot, the President. But in choosing the President, the votes shall be taken by states, the representation from each state having one vote; a quorum for this purpose shall consist of a member or members from two-thirds of the states, and a majority of all the states shall be necessary to a choice. [And if the House of Representatives shall not choose a President whenever the right of choice shall devolve upon them, before the fourth day of March next following, then the Vice-President shall act as President, as in case of the death or other constitutional disability of the President.——]* The person having the greatest number of votes as Vice-President, shall be the Vice-President, if such number be a majority of the whole number of Electors appointed, and if no person have a majority, then from the two highest numbers on the list, the Senate shall choose the Vice-President; a quorum for the purpose shall consist of two-thirds of the whole number of Senators, and a majority of the whole number shall be necessary to a choice. But no person constitutionally ineligible to the office of President shall be eligible to that of Vice-President of the United States.

* Superseded by Section 3 of the Twentieth Amendment.

AMENDMENT XIII

Passed by Congress January 31, 1865. Ratified December 18, 1865.

NOTE: *A portion of Article IV, Section 2, of the Constitution was superseded by the Thirteenth Amendment.*

Section 1

Neither slavery nor involuntary servitude, except as a punishment for crime whereof the party shall have been duly convicted, shall exist within the United States, or any place subject to their jurisdiction.

Section 2

Congress shall have power to enforce this article by appropriate legislation.

AMENDMENT XIV

Passed by Congress June 13, 1866. Ratified July 9, 1868.

NOTE: *Article I, Section 2, of the Constitution was modified by Section 2 of the Fourteenth Amendment.*

Section 1

All persons born or naturalized in the United States, and subject to the jurisdiction thereof, are citizens of the United States and of the State wherein they reside. No State shall make or enforce any law which shall abridge the privileges or immunities of citizens of the United States; nor shall any State deprive any person of life, liberty, or property, without due process of law; nor deny to any person within its jurisdiction the equal protection of the laws.

Section 2

Representatives shall be apportioned among the several States according to their respective numbers, counting the whole number of persons in each State, excluding Indians not taxed. But when the right to vote at any election for the choice of electors for President and Vice-President of the United States, Representatives in Congress, the Executive and Judicial officers of a State, or the members of the Legislature thereof, is denied to any of the male inhabitants of such State, being twenty-one years of age,* and citizens of the United States, or in any way abridged, except for participation in rebellion, or other crime, the basis of representation therein shall be reduced in the proportion which the number of such male citizens shall bear to the whole number of male citizens twenty-one years of age in such State.

Section 3

No person shall be a Senator or Representative in Congress, or elector of President and Vice-President, or hold any office, civil or military, under the United States, or under any State, who, having previously taken an oath, as a member of Congress, or as an officer of the United States, or as a member of any State legislature, or as an executive or judicial officer of any State, to support the Constitution of the United States, shall have engaged in insurrection or rebellion against the same, or given aid or comfort to the enemies thereof. But Congress may by a vote of two-thirds of each House, remove such disability.

Section 4

The validity of the public debt of the United States, authorized by law, including debts incurred for payment of pensions and bounties for services in suppressing insurrection or rebellion, shall not be questioned. But neither the United States nor any State shall assume or pay any debt or obligation incurred in aid of insurrection or rebellion against the United States, or any claim for the loss or emancipation of any slave; but all such debts, obligations and claims shall be held illegal and void.

*Changed by Section 1 of the Twenty-sixth Amendment.

Section 5

The Congress shall have the power to enforce, by appropriate legislation, the provisions of this article.

AMENDMENT XV

Passed by Congress February 26, 1869. Ratified February 3, 1870.

Section 1

The right of citizens of the United States to vote shall not be denied or abridged by the United States or by any State on account of race, color, or previous condition of servitude.

Section 2

The Congress shall have the power to enforce this article by appropriate legislation.

AMENDMENT XVI

Passed by Congress July 2, 1909. Ratified February 3, 1913.

NOTE: *Article I, Section 9, of the Constitution was modified by the Sixteenth Amendment.*

The Congress shall have power to lay and collect taxes on incomes, from whatever source derived, without apportionment among the several States, and without regard to any census or enumeration.

AMENDMENT XVII

Passed by Congress May 13, 1912. Ratified April 8, 1913.

note: *Article I, Section 3, of the Constitution was modified by the Seventeenth Amendment.*

The Senate of the United States shall be composed of two Senators from each State, elected by the people thereof, for six years; and each Senator shall have one vote.

The electors in each State shall have the qualifications requisite for electors of the most numerous branch of the State legislatures.

When vacancies happen in the representation of any State in the Senate, the executive authority of such State shall issue writs of election to fill such vacancies: *Provided*, That the legislature of any State may empower the executive thereof to make temporary appointments until the people fill the vacancies by election as the legislature may direct.

This amendment shall not be so construed as to affect the election or term of any Senator chosen before it becomes valid as part of the Constitution.

AMENDMENT XVIII

Passed by Congress December 18, 1917. Ratified January 16, 1919. Repealed by the Twenty-first Amendment.

Section 1

After one year from the ratification of this article the manufacture, sale, or transportation of intoxicating liquors within, the importation thereof into, or the exportation thereof from the United States and all territory subject to the jurisdiction thereof for beverage purposes is hereby prohibited.

Section 2

The Congress and the several States shall have concurrent power to enforce this article by appropriate legislation.

Section 3

This article shall be inoperative unless it shall have been ratified as an amendment to the Constitution by the legislatures of the several States, as provided in the Constitution, within seven years from the date of the submission hereof to the States by the Congress.

AMENDMENT XIX

Passed by Congress June 4, 1919. Ratified August 18, 1920.

The right of citizens of the United States to vote shall not be denied or abridged by the United States or by any State on account of sex.

Congress shall have power to enforce this article by appropriate legislation.

AMENDMENT XX

Passed by Congress March 2, 1932. Ratified January 23, 1933.

NOTE: *Article I, Section 4, of the Constitution was modified by Section 2 of this amendment. In addition, a portion of the Twelfth Amendment was superseded by Section 3.*

Section 1

The terms of the President and the Vice President shall end at noon on the 20th day of January, and the terms of Senators and Representatives at noon on the 3d day of January, of the years in which such terms would have ended if this article had not been ratified; and the terms of their successors shall then begin.

Section 2

The Congress shall assemble at least once in every year, and such meeting shall begin at noon on the 3d day of January, unless they shall by law appoint a different day.

Section 3

If, at the time fixed for the beginning of the term of the President, the President elect shall have died, the Vice President elect shall become President. If a President shall not have been chosen before the time fixed for the beginning of his term, or if the President elect shall have failed to qualify, then the Vice President elect shall act as President until a President shall have qualified; and the Congress may by law provide for the case wherein neither a President elect nor a Vice President shall have qualified, declaring who shall then act as President, or the manner in which one who is to act shall be selected, and such person shall act accordingly until a President or Vice President shall have qualified.

Section 4

The Congress may by law provide for the case of the death of any of the persons from whom the House of Representatives may choose a President whenever the right of choice shall have devolved upon them, and for the case of the death of any of the persons from whom the Senate may choose a Vice President whenever the right of choice shall have devolved upon them.

Section 5

Sections 1 and 2 shall take effect on the 15th day of October following the ratification of this article.

Section 6

This article shall be inoperative unless it shall have been ratified as an amendment to the Constitution by the legislatures of three-fourths of the several States within seven years from the date of its submission.

AMENDMENT XXI

Passed by Congress February 20, 1933. Ratified December 5, 1933.

Section 1

The eighteenth article of amendment to the Constitution of the United States is hereby repealed.

Section 2

The transportation or importation into any State, Territory, or Possession of the United States for delivery or use therein of intoxicating liquors, in violation of the laws thereof, is hereby prohibited.

Section 3

This article shall be inoperative unless it shall have been ratified as an amendment to the Constitution by conventions in the several States, as provided in the Constitution, within seven years from the date of the submission hereof to the States by the Congress.

AMENDMENT XXII

Passed by Congress March 21, 1947. Ratified February 27, 1951.

Section 1

No person shall be elected to the office of the President more than twice, and no person who has held the office of President, or acted as President, for more than two years of a term to which some other person was elected President shall be elected to the office of President more than once. But this Article shall not apply to any person holding the office of President when this Article was proposed by Congress, and shall not prevent any person who may be holding the office of President, or acting as President, during the term within which this Article becomes operative from holding the office of President or acting as President during the remainder of such term.

Section 2

This article shall be inoperative unless it shall have been ratified as an amendment to the Constitution by the legislatures of three-fourths of the several States within seven years from the date of its submission to the States by the Congress.

AMENDMENT XXIII

Passed by Congress June 16, 1960. Ratified March 29, 1961.

Section 1

The District constituting the seat of Government of the United States shall appoint in such manner as Congress may direct:

A number of electors of President and Vice President equal to the whole number of Senators and Representatives in Congress to which the District would be entitled if it were a State, but in no event more than the least populous State; they shall be in addition to those appointed by the States, but they shall be considered, for the purposes of the election of President and Vice President, to be electors appointed by a State; and they shall meet in the District and perform such duties as provided by the twelfth article of amendment.

Section 2

The Congress shall have power to enforce this article by appropriate legislation.

Amendment XXIV

Passed by Congress August 27, 1962. Ratified January 23, 1964.

Section 1

The right of citizens of the United States to vote in any primary or other election for President or Vice President, for electors for President or Vice President, or for Senator or Representative in Congress, shall not be denied or abridged by the United States or by any State by reason of failure to pay poll tax or other tax.

Section 2

The Congress shall have power to enforce this article by appropriate legislation.

Amendment XXV

Passed by Congress July 6, 1965. Ratified February 10, 1967.

NOTE: *Article II, Section 1, of the Constitution was affected by the Twenty-fifth Amendment.*

Section 1

In case of the removal of the President from office or of his death or resignation, the Vice President shall become President.

Section 2

Whenever there is a vacancy in the office of the Vice President, the President shall nominate a Vice President who shall take office upon confirmation by a majority vote of both Houses of Congress.

Section 3

Whenever the President transmits to the President pro tempore of the Senate and the Speaker of the House of Representatives his written declaration that he is unable to discharge the powers and duties of his office, and until he transmits to them a written declaration to the contrary, such powers and duties shall be discharged by the Vice President as Acting President.

Section 4

Whenever the Vice President and a majority of either the principal officers of the executive departments or of such other body as Congress may by law provide, transmit to the President pro tempore of the Senate and the Speaker of the House of Representatives their written declaration that the President is unable to discharge the powers and duties of his office, the Vice President shall immediately assume the powers and duties of the office as Acting President.

Thereafter, when the President transmits to the President pro tempore of the Senate and the Speaker of the House of Representatives his written declaration that no inability exists, he shall resume the powers and duties of his office unless the Vice President and a majority of either the principal officers of the executive department or of such other body as Congress may by law provide, transmit within four days to the President pro tempore of the Senate and the Speaker of the House of Representatives their written declaration that the President is unable to discharge the powers and duties of his office. Thereupon Congress shall decide the issue, assembling within forty-eight hours for that purpose if not in session. If the Congress, within twenty-one days after receipt of the latter written declaration, or, if Congress is not in session, within twenty-one days after Congress is required to assemble, determines by two-thirds vote of both Houses that the President is unable to discharge the powers and duties of his office, the Vice President shall continue to discharge the same as Acting President; otherwise, the President shall resume the powers and duties of his office.

AMENDMENT XXVI

Passed by Congress March 23, 1971. Ratified July 1, 1971.

NOTE: *Amendment XIV, Section 2, of the Constitution was modified by Section 1 of the Twenty-sixth Amendment.*

Section 1

The right of citizens of the United States, who are eighteen years of age or older, to vote shall not be denied or abridged by the United States or by any State on account of age.

Section 2

The Congress shall have power to enforce this article by appropriate legislation.

AMENDMENT XXVII

Originally proposed Sept. 25, 1789. Ratified May 7, 1992.

No law, varying the compensation for the services of the Senators and Representatives, shall take effect, until an election of representatives shall have intervened.

APPENDIX H

The Emancipation Proclamation

· ·

January 1, 1863

By the President of the United States of America:

A PROCLAMATION.

Whereas, on the twenty-second day of September, in the year of our Lord one thousand eight hundred and sixty-two, a proclamation was issued by the President of the United States, containing, among other things, the following, to wit:

"That on the first day of January, in the year of our Lord one thousand eight hundred and sixty-three, all persons held as slaves within any State or designated part of a State, the people whereof shall then be in rebellion against the United States, shall be then, thenceforward, and forever free; and the Executive Government of the United States, including the military and naval authority thereof, will recognize and maintain the freedom of such persons, and will do no act or acts to repress such persons, or any of them, in any efforts they may make for their actual freedom.

"That the Executive will, on the first day of January aforesaid, by proclamation, designate the States and parts of States, if any, in which the people thereof, respectively, shall then be in rebellion against the United States; and the fact that any State, or the people thereof, shall on that day be, in good faith, represented in the Congress of the United States by members chosen thereto at elections wherein a majority of the qualified voters of such State shall have participated, shall, in the absence of strong countervailing testimony, be deemed conclusive evidence that such State, and the people thereof, are not then in rebellion against the United States."

Now, therefore I, Abraham Lincoln, President of the United States, by virtue of the power in me vested as Commander-in-Chief, of the Army and Navy of the United States in time of actual armed rebellion against the authority and government of the United States, and as a fit and necessary war measure for suppressing said rebellion, do, on this first day of January, in the year of our Lord one thousand eight hundred and sixty-three, and in accordance with my purpose so to do publicly proclaimed for the full period of one hundred days, from the day first above mentioned, order and designate as the States and parts of States wherein the people thereof respectively, are this day in rebellion against the United States, the following, to wit:

Arkansas, Texas, Louisiana, (except the Parishes of St. Bernard, Plaquemines, Jefferson, St. John, St. Charles, St. James Ascension, Assumption, Terrebonne, Lafourche, St. Mary, St. Martin, and Orleans, including the City of New Orleans) Mississippi, Alabama, Florida, Georgia, South Carolina, North Carolina, and Virginia, (except the forty-eight counties designated as West Virginia, and also the counties of Berkley, Accomac, Northampton, Elizabeth City, York, Princess Ann, and Norfolk, including the cities of Norfolk and Portsmouth[)], and which excepted parts, are for the present, left precisely as if this proclamation were not issued.

And by virtue of the power, and for the purpose aforesaid, I do order and declare that all persons held as slaves within said designated States, and parts of States, are, and henceforward shall be free; and that the Executive government of the United States, including the military and naval authorities thereof, will recognize and maintain the freedom of said persons.

And I hereby enjoin upon the people so declared to be free to abstain from all violence, unless in necessary self-defence; and I recommend to them that, in all cases when allowed, they labor faithfully for reasonable wages.

And I further declare and make known, that such persons of suitable condition, will be received into the armed service of the United States to garrison forts, positions, stations, and other places, and to man vessels of all sorts in said service.

And upon this act, sincerely believed to be an act of justice, warranted by the Constitution, upon military necessity, I invoke the considerate judgment of mankind, and the gracious favor of Almighty God.

In witness whereof, I have hereunto set my hand and caused the seal of the United States to be affixed.

Done at the City of Washington, this first day of January, in the year of our Lord one thousand eight hundred and sixty three, and of the Independence of the United States of America the eighty-seventh.

By the President: ABRAHAM LINCOLN

WILLIAM H. SEWARD, Secretary of State.

Index